T0265711

"Founding a business is heroic. It takes vision and fortitude. Founders ignite businesses, but do not always have the skills to scale the business they created. This is where *The Second CEO* comes in. With complimentary skills and attributes, the Second CEO drives the business to fulfill its potential. This book gives any CEO following a founder the insights and playbook for success. Matt Sharrers brings acute understanding and years of relevant experience to this important topic."

SIMON FREAKLEY, CEO, Alix Partners

"Following a founder is one of the toughest challenges a new CEO can face, and there's little guidance for how to do it. Matt Sharrers is the first to offer a clear path and proven approach for how to succeed. His advice is simple, practical, and powerful. Every Second CEO will benefit from reading this book and applying its hard-earned lessons."

RANDY STREET, Vice Chairman, GH Smart

"As investors in dozens of founder-operated businesses, we have witnessed first-hand the fraught nature of transitioning to the Second CEO. Even when everyone is operating with good intentions, there is a sense of flying into the unknown and of navigating by intuition. Based on authentic, courageous reflection on his own experiences, Matt has written the definitive guide to getting this transition right. At Resolve, this book will serve as the platinum standard in our role as board members and investors to help a Second CEO accelerate through the scaling process."

JIT SINHA, Founder, Managing Partner, Resolve Growth

"Matt is uniquely qualified to share his experiences following a founder and transitioning his business into a professionally run organization. Matt's passion, energy, leadership style, and 'scorecard' approach to an organization all come out in this important book that is a fantastic read. The different case studies and experiences he shares shows that following a founder is never straight forward, but the lessons he and others learned can help setup a Second CEO for a successful transition. As a private equity investor and board member on many founder-run companies over the past twenty years, I wish I had access to this book years ago!"

JUSTIN LIPTON, Partner, Co-Head, Harvest Partners

The SECOND
CEO

The *SECOND* CEO

CEO

Accelerating Scale
WHEN FOLLOWING
the Founder

MATT SHARRERS

Advantage | Books

Published by Advantage Books, Charleston, South Carolina.
An imprint of Advantage Media.

ADVANTAGE is a registered trademark, and the Advantage colophon is a trademark of Advantage Media Group, Inc.

Printed in the United States of America.

10 9 8 7 6 5 4 3 2 1

ISBN: 978-1-64225-939-1 (Hardcover)
ISBN: 978-1-64225-938-4 (eBook)

Library of Congress Control Number: 2024904623

Book design by Wesley Strickland.

This publication is designed to provide accurate and authoritative information in regard to the subject matter covered. It is sold with the understanding that the publisher is not engaged in rendering legal, accounting, or other professional services. If legal advice or other expert assistance is required, the services of a competent professional person should be sought.

Advantage Books is an imprint of Advantage Media Group. Advantage Media helps busy entrepreneurs, CEOs, and leaders write and publish a book to grow their business and become the authority in their field. Advantage authors comprise an exclusive community of industry professionals, idea-makers, and thought leaders. For more information go to **advantagemedia.com**.

This book is dedicated to the greatest coaches I have ever had.

Barb Sharrers: Thank you, Mom. You demonstrated every soft skill that elite CEOs need to have: consistent empathy, unsurpassed selflessness, and a wonderful sense of humor that ensures nobody ever takes themselves too seriously.

Dan Sharrers: My father and the most inspiring leader I have ever witnessed. Polarizing command, authentic wisdom, and an unquenchable curiosity about who people are but more importantly, who they can become. Thank you for reminding me every day to enjoy the journey. I miss you every day.

Lynne Sharrers: My amazing wife. Thank you for your countless sacrifices. Leaving your career enabled us to go all in on SBI in the early days. Watching you raise our four wonderful children is a daily lesson in what it takes to lead. Thank you for your belief in me, your unconditional love and support, especially when I didn't deserve it. You inspire me every day to be better.

CONTENTS

ACKNOWLEDGMENTS

It takes so many people to write a book, yet often times the author is the one who gets the credit. This book did not happen without contributions and insights from many. I am truly humbled and honored these people were on this journey with me.

Tim Stratman: Thank you for being more than I could have imagined as an executive coach. You were always there to support me and knew just the right thing to say to keep me centered over my time as a CEO when so many of these lessons were learned. You are as good as they get, my friend.

Greg Alexander: The founder I followed. An authentic friend and mentor who has always been in my corner encouraging me to reach for my full potential.

Aaron Bartels, Mike Drapeau, John Staples, and Scott Gruher: I cannot think of four people I would share a foxhole with more than you. I appreciate you believing in me when the road was blurry and pushing me to become a better version of T1. Our lives transformed together, and what a journey it was.

Scott Marden and Justin Lipton: CIP Capital made a big bet on SBI and Matt Sharrers. You were great partners when things were good and even better when things were bumpy. I appreciate your conviction on our firm.

Mary Martin: I was unsure what to expect when I started thinking about working with a ghostwriter. You were much more than that: a strategic thinking partner, idea generator, keeper of so many interview notes where nuggets of insight were buried … and you always showed up to every working session with a smile and boundless energy. You are a pro, and other authors should be honored to work with you.

To all of the founders, Second CEOs, and private equity investors who so readily shared their time and insight for this book: "Thank you" seems significantly less than you all deserve for your contributions. Hopefully, the readers will appreciate your advice as much as I did.

To my brother Jay: The most loyal and loving brother a guy could ever ask for. Appreciate you, pal, for being who you are. Keep inspiring your tribe to reach their full potential. Mom and Dad are so proud of you.

To Landon, Sydney, Cierra, and Ella, our four incredible children. Thank you for inspiring me to live our family value of Ambition to its fullest. For reminding me to chill a little bit more often. Keeping me young with all of your college drinking games and making me prouder than words can ever possibly convey. You give Mom and I a sense of purpose that will only make sense to you when you become parents. I love you.

FOREWORD

My name is Greg Alexander. I was the founder who hired Matt Sharrers, the author of this book. He was the Second CEO following the founder.

I trusted him to accelerate and scale what was once "my baby,"
In your hands is the methodology he used to do it.

This book is a success story. If you want to learn how to follow a founder, being the Second CEO, you are about to read the very best book on this subject. There are no books that truly exist on how to fill the shoes of a founder, how to take a company to the next level once the founder has stepped aside.

This book is not a cautionary tale, and this is what makes it different. The author wastes none of your time. He assumes you understand the challenges you face and gets right to the solution immediately. Two hours with this book equates to twenty hours with another.

And here is the best part: this book is about you. It is not about the author. Matt does not need to establish his credibility. Ask around. His reputation, in impressive circles, is flawless. Therefore, he does not waste your time rehashing the glory days because he understands you don't care about him. You care about you. And so, Matt gets to the point, and you are the beneficiary.

Why should you take my word for it?

Matt followed me, no one else. I am speaking from first-hand experience. The baton was passed from one person, me, to one person, Matt. If you are trying to decide if you should read this book, ignore everyone else's opinion. They were not there. They did not live it. And therefore, they are speculating. I am the horse. And my recommendation comes directly from the horse's mouth. If you are following a founder as a company's Second CEO, read this book. Twice.

Still not sure if this book is worth your time?

Consider this.

I am very hard to work for, and impossible to succeed. Yet, the author did so successfully. And this fact, more than any other, is why I feel you should read this book.

My employees named me after the most iconic villain ever in popular culture, Darth Vader. I was a cyborg, who cared only about one thing: results. To work for me was to go to war with victory as the only acceptable outcome to death. Employees avoided me, and most hated me. To be in my proximity was to be pushed to the extremes. Yes, I am crazy. I can feel you judging me. You are not the first.

Yet, despite this, one employee, the author, jumped in every foxhole with me. One employee, Matt Sharrers, charged up every hill with me, shoulder to shoulder, as the bullets buzzed by. As my ambition expanded, and I needed help, I trusted one person: the author. And so, when it came time to trust someone with the entire firm, there was only one choice. Matt Sharrers became the firm's Second CEO in August of 2017.

This story is relevant to you because you are following a founder. Founders are crazy. And you are signing up to follow one. I bet he or she is just as nuts and difficult as I am. You need to know what you are getting into. And Matt is the best person to make sure you pull this off. Why? He did what you are about to do. And I would argue that he did it under more severe conditions than you, more than most. His methodology is battle tested.

So, in closing, make the decision to read this book. It will be the best decision you will make all year.

With much respect and admiration,

GREG ALEXANDER

Cofounder, SBI

Founder, Collective 54

INTRODUCTION

I've had three distinct careers, and they've all been around high performance. First, I was a hockey player. I was fortunate to play a game I love for a living and get a taste of a life where high performance on a daily basis determines your success or failure. When I retired, I started my business career, quickly rising up the ranks to become the vice president/corporate officer before my thirty-fourth birthday at a Fortune 500 company. From there, I joined Sales Benchmark Index (SBI), a GTM strategy consulting firm, as its first employee, working alongside its three cofounders. We scaled SBI into one of the largest boutique firms in go-to-market consulting over fifteen years, including two liquidity events.

But all wasn't always rosy. During my eighth year with SBI, our cofounder and CEO, Greg Alexander, was getting antsy. He was ready to do his next thing. SBI was no longer giving Greg's entrepreneurial spirit what it needed. At this point, we had six partners who all had ownership. He let us know he wanted to exit SBI. The partners agreed that I should be his successor. Great, right? Well, not so much. In theory, it sounded fantastic—I was about to follow the founder and be the new CEO! But in practice, there was no playbook. My first year could have been much more methodical and with many less mistakes. So here we are.

This is the book I wish I had back in 2016, when Greg first announced he wanted to step away. We had to do it all by trial and error. And yes, we got to a great outcome. But you don't have to repeat our mistakes because you'll know where the landmines are and how to avoid them.

A lot has been written about succession. But taking over for a founder-CEO is its own, unique type of succession that happens only once. It's hard enough to replace a CEO, but there's an extra degree of difficulty when you're following a founder. That difficulty has elements of personality, culture, and history that can easily derail the entire transition if they aren't handled well. And if the founder is going to continue to be involved, the resulting dynamic can be even more challenging.

If you're the person who has been tapped on the shoulder to succeed the CEO, you need a plan. You need a step-by-step guide for navigating the situation and preparing yourself to follow the founder. Even if you're already in the position, you need a way to check your progress. As important, you need to execute in a way that supports relationships and professionalizes the business while accelerating scale.

Meanwhile, you could be in a company where succession is starting to be talked about and you may be wondering, *Am I the right person?* And if you think you are, how do you position yourself? What's your next best move? And the one after that?

If you are or might be following a founder, I've been in your shoes. And if you're a founder-CEO who needs to find a successor, I understand. I have had the privilege as part of my CEO coaching business to execute on multiple founder successions. Even if you're on the board of a company with a founder-CEO who's about to exit, or you coach a founder-CEO who's lost that loving feeling for the job, I've been in your shoes. All of those experiences were on-the-job training for the creation of my current business: *helping the Second CEO accelerate scale when following the founder.*

If you're reading this book, you know that the personality of a founder doesn't always map onto the prototypical CEO profile. Founders are one-of-a-kind: prolific, dynamic, engaging, and inspiring. Many aren't classically trained in running a business. In fact, part of their DNA is ideation to *start a business and solve a problem.* Many of them often wish they didn't have to operate and manage the company they started. But it comes with the territory, especially in professional services. What they lack in training, they make up for in vision and ideas. They can be charismatic, dramatic, and larger than life. Following someone like that can be very difficult.

Nevertheless, the growth and success of the company hinge on getting this transition right. The future health of the relationships of the key players and everyone else in the company is at stake. Jobs, work relationships, the stress on the families of those involved, financials, business success . . . they're all more fragile than you might think, and succession makes them all extremely vulnerable. It's not hyperbole to say that getting this one transition wrong could destroy everything everyone has worked hard to build.

I've been fortunate to have coached and mentored dozens of CEOs over my career. Furthermore, with twenty-five years spent in boardrooms and PE firm diligence meetings, I've seen and witnessed some succession decisions that were masterful. And I've seen many that blew up. Some were founders whose replacements I helped pick, and others were the replacements following the founders. I've also been in the position of replacing myself—a first employee of a firm.

In retrospect, that was a decision requiring a certain kind of attention that I was unaware of at the time.

The stories in this book (all true, although some have been made unidentifiable) contain cautionary tales, someone who hit it out of the park with no outside coaching, and someone who had to quickly be replaced and have the founder step back in after the initial replacement took the company significantly backward. If you want to hit it out of the park, use this book as your road map.

On the following pages, I'll guide you through your thoughts, feelings, and actions, from the moment you're tapped on the shoulder as the successor or the external search has identified you as a match through the actual transition and your first year as CEO. I'll provide you with:

- ☑ Guidance for your transition out of your position, if you are internal, and into CEO, including how to handle filling the gap you're creating when you move into your new position.

- ☑ How to create value when the entire company has grown accustomed to the personality and practices (for good or not) of one person.

- ☑ A detailed operating road map of the first quarter and the first year when you follow a founder.

- ☑ Guidance for identifying *your* team versus *the* team.

- ☑ A process for creating and managing a board.

- ☑ Guidance on how to properly manage a private equity/VC firm if you're taking over a business owned by these investors.

- ☑ *Key Accelerants,* which are tips for accelerating scale when following a founder.

As you read *The Second CEO: Accelerating Scale When Following the Founder,* you'll notice the chapters have a natural linearity to them. But this book isn't intended to be a step-by-step, sequential guide. Instead, it's a guide for what you need to get right in your first year. Some stops on your journey won't need much time and others will, depending on your unique circumstances. And some areas need immediate attention, regardless of what chapter I address them in. For example, you're not going to ignore urgent people decisions that need to be made thirty days in just because I don't go deep into talent until chapter 9. Keep a mindset of agility.

Here's what to expect:

Chapter 1 tells the story that was the impetus for this book. It's a cautionary tale about me fumbling my way through following a founder. Also in chapter 1 is one of my favorite stories about a powerhouse founder whose self-awareness, business acumen, and humility were the perfect combination to lead to a successful transition to a Second CEO.

Chapter 2 acknowledges the only thing likely on your mind right now: *Am I ready?* Whatever is happening with you internally is OK, and this chapter will get you to where you need to be.

Chapter 3 is chock full of stories and advice for working with the founder. It also includes leadership styles, inviting you to reflect on the founder you're following as well as the kind of leader you want to be.

Chapter 4 launches you into the firsts: the first days, weeks, and months. You'll begin with a Listening Tour where you'll be getting a feel for what's going well, what (and who!) needs to go, and what you might need to start doing. You never stop listening, but this particular time is intensive and strategic.

Chapter 5 discusses purpose, vision, values, and culture, which drive behavior and cohesiveness of teams. Accelerating scale can only occur when there's alignment on these crucial cornerstones of your company's ecosystem.

Chapter 6 describes my take on strategy and the Two-Horizon model I recommend.

Chapter 7 dives into processes and the need to get them documented before you move on to . . .

Chapter 8 explains your organizational structure. We'll be referring to roles, not people, here, as that's the way to get structure right.

Chapter 9 is all about team building, understanding who you have, who you need, and what it will take to make them a high-performing, cohesive team.

Chapter 10 coaches you through your relationship with the board. And if you don't have one, I'll show you how to create one.

PASSING THE BATON VERSUS THROWING IT AND RUNNING

*The Importance of Setting Up the
Second CEO for Success*

If you're reading this book, you're the person who could be the next CEO. Maybe you already work for the company and maybe you don't. Regardless, there's no such thing as thinking too much about the transition from founder to Second CEO. If you're not prepared for the transition, the consequences could be dire, personally, professionally, and financially. This moment is perhaps the most underappreciated, undervalued moment in the history of succession. And yet, it's the most consequential.

The best way to communicate just how consequential this moment is, is through real-life stories. And in my mind, there's no better story to begin with than the one that compelled me to write *The Second CEO*—where I was thrown the baton. There was no playbook for this decisive moment in the life of a business and I made a lot of mistakes. Once I figured it all out, I was determined to do my part to build a repeatable system versus figuring it out along the way. The latter characterized my first experience following a founder.

Case Study #1: Greg and Me

I was the first employee at SBI, a strategy consulting firm that specialized in go-to-market effectiveness. I followed Greg Alexander, Aaron Bartels, and Mike Drapeau. The company was growing, and Greg, our CEO, started to feel that entrepreneurial urge in year seven. Greg has true founder DNA, which I'll discuss in depth in the next chapter. For now, what that looks like is a passion for starting things.

Greg was delegating more and more to me because he was getting frustrated and looking for a path out. Although I didn't have a lot of experience, I was resourceful, I learned quickly, I could figure anything out, and I got along with people. So me stepping up worked for everyone but didn't solve the actual problem, which was that Greg wanted to keep innovating and felt like the firm (his two cofounders, employees, and clients) was holding him back. As you might imagine, this created a lot of conflict internally.

But that was just half the problem. The other half was there was no coherent strategy or consistent direction. That created confusion, which led to a lot of staff turnover. Realistically, we were just making things up as we went along. We had no grand plan with a timeline, benchmarks, and what we were agreeing to do or not do as a business. We didn't have one clear, unified message internally, and although we were still growing and making money, that was pretty much due to luck.

The interpersonal tensions from that time took such a toll that we went from being like a brotherhood to being disappointed with each other to anger and resentment to now, where our relationships have been fractured permanently. As of writing this book, I'm happy to share that my friendships with Greg, Aaron, and Mike are intact. I am forever indebted to the three of them for starting SBI and taking a chance on me two years into the journey.

The trigger event that prompted the change was we knew Greg wanted out. We found a way to make that happen while allowing the rest of us to continue to grow the firm. Because valuations for professional services firms had increased significantly, Greg could sell his equity to us, move on, and we could retain control of the firm.

Looking back seven years later, Greg selling his equity was a good move as it started a path to each of the founders monetizing their equity and creating generational wealth. At the same time, I think it's fair to say no one behaved like their best selves during that process. And a lot of that comes back to the fact that we didn't have a playbook. What the business needed was a consistent, methodical operator to standardize what we were doing and scale it. And of course, it needed a process for succession.

Greg and the partners chose me to succeed him because they thought I was the right person. But we didn't think through what might happen internally or how to best pass the torch. I was leap-frogging over the other two founders, and despite their public support, they had natural hesitation and concern behind the scenes. We were naive and inexperienced yet managed to buy Greg's shares by bringing in an investor (Alaris Royalty) at a number that made him happy and we could live with. Yes, we got a deal done, but not because we knew what we were doing, and not before creating chaos.

The transition was not smooth from the start. This was nobody's fault. I had never done this before. Nor had Greg. In year eleven, Greg and I went to Dallas for a day and a half and, rapid-fire, he gave me a crash course in all the functional things he owned that would now be my job. And all of that *doing* was his way—the way he had done things. This isn't his fault or mine. We were scrappy entrepreneurs, and the way to transition is to have the person leaving tell you all the things they were doing. He needed to make sure I understood what my job was. And then two days later, we announce, "Greg's leaving and Matt's the CEO." Boom, I get shot out of a cannon and now I'm running the company and Greg is gone. This is *not* how to do things. And the mistakes didn't end there.

There I am, *suddenly CEO*, making mistakes of my own, beginning with not being cognizant of the fact that a Matt-led SBI is different from a Greg-led SBI. I was trying to be a derivative of Greg, and I didn't give myself any space to find my own unique style. And because we're different people with different gaps, we need different executive leadership teams. But I just pushed forward and made changes, like putting someone in the position I left vacant because I liked him. I didn't ask myself: *How do I purposefully move through leadership changes to not break the organization, and do it at the right pace?* Nope, there was none of that.

Instead of slow-playing it and taking three months to sit back, talk to clients and employees about the current state of things, listen to their thoughts and concerns, and create and lay out a strategy, I jumped in like I owned the place. I did too much too soon, making a lot of changes and putting my stamp on things. We had too many initiatives, and I was unable to succinctly focus on the business. We whipsawed and I distracted the firm. *This is a priority! And this is a priority! And this, too! Sell, sell, sell!* I was acting like a super sales leader, as opposed to a CEO.

My reckoning came at month six, when I was coming back from a business trip to New York. I got a note from Aaron that we were going to be entering a tough stretch for the firm. We had debt payments to make to our investor and some of the spending decisions I had made had not yet resulted in financial lift. To mitigate this and stay in compliance, we had to lay off 10 percent of the firm. We had a new investor, so that changed our operating cadence, covenants, and how we had to act. We were skating very closely to crossing our covenants, which I had no real appreciation for—yet another Year One gap. We had to step back and do that even though we knew it would be challenging. It was very painful, personally and professionally. People lost their jobs. People lost confidence. I lost confidence and hit a professional low. *Am I right for this?*

That's when clarity came for me. It's unfortunate that wreckage came first, but we got our bearings as a leadership team. I got my bearings as a CEO and identified my priorities. I knew, and our investor firm knew, that my time as CEO would be six years, maximum. I had always wanted to be out of operating roles by my fiftieth birthday, so I had an expiration date. I was forty-four at the time. Given that timeline, I knew I would be the firm's leader for five to six years and then transition to someone to follow me. I was deeply motivated to establish a process that corrected for the havoc I was part of and partly caused. I didn't want history to repeat itself.

The fix for my situation began with hiring the leadership assessment firm ghSMART to assess me as a CEO and identify my gaps. Then I found a coach to work with to help me fill those gaps. Next, Aaron and I agreed we needed a management method to run the firm.

We chose Scaling Up from Verne Harnish. Finally, I needed what's called a *scorecard*, which details what the CEO of *this* company does, and where they're going.

The scorecard concept started with Dr. Brad Smart, whose son Geoff took it to a new level at his firm. Geoff is a pioneer in the field of leadership assessment and his firm is now a top leadership advisory firm, frequently landing at number one on lists of management consulting companies. Geoff and his now vice chairman, Randy Street, coauthored the *New York Times* bestseller *Who: A Method for Hiring* nearly fifteen years ago, and it remains a powerful book on the importance of choosing the right people.

In *Who,* Geoff and Randy write: "The scorecard is a document that describes exactly what you want a person to accomplish in a role. It is not a job description, but rather a set of outcomes and competencies that define a job done well."

A good scorecard process translates the objectives of the strategy into clear outcomes for the CEO and senior leadership team.

The power of the scorecard lies not only in its clarity and transparency but in its use as an accountability tool and a vehicle for the most important part of your role: professionalizing the business by creating repeatable systems and processes that clear the path for ease of scaling.

The scorecard brought a lot of structure and discipline to how to operate a business as a CEO and I use it with all the CEOs I coach. A scorecard is a critical first move to focus on the business. Only after you have it can you even think about what operations should look like, how to lead, and how to scale.

This is only one portion of my story with SBI, but it's part of the impetus for this book. The second part of the story is after this unfortunate experience the firm returned to growth. We grew year over year and hit a major milestone in 2020: selling a majority stake to a private equity firm, CIP Capital. Scaling a professional services firm is hard. Doing it at a level where disciplined investors who look at hundreds of potential companies in which to invest for every one they do is a true accomplishment. At the time of the transaction, there were seven partners in the firm including me. Aaron, Mike, John Staples, Scott Gruher, Eric Estrella, and Josh Horstmann. I will forever be connected to these six incredible guys—as a former athlete, it was the equivalent of winning a championship. While some retired, some stayed, and some did new things, we did something very few firms do. We actually did it twice in less than four years. And our second time, we had four offers. We were blessed to get a premium and this triggered a path of wealth generation for not only us but many early SBI employees. I was so honored to lead this tribe.

I'll unpack all of my lessons in a bit, but for now know that when you're taking over from a founder, whether you come from the inside of the company or not, you need to operate as if you don't. I'll be repeating that throughout the book; that's how crucial it is. You can't just dive into action. You have to give yourself time and the team time to acclimate.

Case Study #2: Kristie and Eric

The flip side of my situation with SBI is Bespoke Partners, an executive search firm that specializes in private equity software. The founder Kristie Nova asked me to be on the board a few years ago with one of my primary responsibilities being to help her create a succession plan. For starters, it's rare for a founder of a privately held boutique to proactively go out and build a board. Kristie recruited me and two other senior executives to be on her board.

As Kristie tells the story, "We always had the belief that the money would come if we lived our values and got things done as a team. People first, always do the right thing, and overinvest in the team." Her style was to be direct, open, and honest, and know where her limits were. Kristie knew she didn't want a lifestyle business. The goal was to scale the firm to a point where there would be enough value to have a liquidity event and move Bespoke to a new level.

About six years into the journey, there were too many signs that the firm had an overreliance on her. From business development to client challenges to human capital issues, it was becoming exhausting. This fatigue was magnified because these were operational issues that didn't play to the strengths of most founders. Sure, the business funded a great lifestyle, but cultural implications were emerging. When Bespoke grew from twenty-five to seventy-five people, Kristie's role became more internally focused. She didn't like that and everyone noticed.

She put her hand up for help and asked me to help find her a successor. And she was deliberate in choosing me. Bespoke needed a CEO who had operating skills, who had followed a founder, and who had sold a company. There were two other roles we needed on the board. First, an organizational specialist for internal assessments and coaching with a human capital background. This was Andy Caine. Lastly, we needed someone who could help build operational process and be a strategic voice. This was Eric Palmer. The board came together quickly in the service of Bespoke's five-year plan to get to its next big milestone and then step aside.

Our first order of business was to create a scorecard for the job of CEO. We're not talking about what Kristie ended up doing, but what the CEO of Bespoke Partners *should be* doing. And then we did a search to identify potential matches to assess according to the scorecard. Either the candidate was a match or not. But then we went a step further, into cultural implications. No one knows what's going to happen with the new person, no matter how perfect a match they are according to the scorecard. Even if they're from within, we don't know how the rest of the people are going to respond to that person in the CEO role. This unknown is tricky, and as you'll see, it can lead to unexpected results.

Remember when Tim Cook took over after Steve Jobs in August of 2011? So many people were proclaiming the end of Apple for a variety of reasons, one of which was: no one else could inspire people like Jobs could. But did everyone quit because they didn't find Tim Cook inspiring? And did the world turn its back on Apple because without Steve Jobs it wasn't as cool? Not even close. Since Cook took over as CEO in 2011, Apple's stock has returned 1,212 percent versus 290 percent for the S&P 500.

Our search for a scorecard-match for Bespoke Partners landed on Eric Walczykowski, who had energy for ideation and the kind of objectivity that would allow him to figure out what the business needed, and do that without emotion. He would come on board as president and COO with a twelve- to eighteen-month succession plan to CEO.

We all knew the team would need to fully embrace Eric, and that suddenly switching to a new CEO was out of the question. She loved those people and was heavily invested. And they loved her back. It was a little bit bumpy culturally for a bit, and then it smoothed out. She had so much confidence in Eric that no one doubted he was the right person for the job.

I can't overstate the importance of a CEO fully embracing somebody like Eric and being completely confident in his abilities. There were still bumps in the road, largely because Eric was professionalizing the business and had no emotional ties to "the good old days." These nostalgic elements from the founder-led business are impossible to recreate. But Eric was able to appreciate the war stories and other shared memories in the context of an evolving Bespoke. Meanwhile, Kristie embraced the need for change and had no issue letting go. Within sixteen months of him becoming president, the firm had a liquidity event, Eric became the CEO, and the torch was passed.

Takeaways from Case Studies #1 and #2

The crucial lessons in these cases have little to do with money. Bespoke and SBI are examples of founders reaching a major milestone.

Here are my takeaways after having a front seat to both transitions.

Self-awareness is vital to a successful transition, but it's not enough. In both outlined cases, two founders knew they were not satisfied and needed to do something else.

Having a clear plan for transition is key. Many founders don't think about the "exit" phase of their operating role as the CEO. It will happen. And usually faster than you think.

Culture matters, and it must evolve. Founder-led businesses are different in that they tend to allow far more experimentation and a general mindset of *figuring it out*. The founder might go through periods of mission drift or not ever appear to be focused on one thing. And that's not a fault; it's who they are as visionaries. But if they want to scale and create value, they need to evolve, and they need to bring the culture along with them. The successful founder-CEO transition involves a methodical evolution toward systems and processes driven by a great executive team. This cultural evolution cannot be overlooked.

When you have a solid transition plan, it makes a world of difference to the internal stability of the company. The Bespoke board knew Eric could not just pop in one day and take over. We knew what would have to happen and how, and the whole company needed to see that in addition to Eric's core business skills.

Founders have entrepreneurship in their DNA. They want to start things and they're constantly innovating, at least in their heads. If they're not in a position where they have the freedom to act on their nature, everybody suffers.

There's a difference between a new CEO coming from within and from outside. But either way, that person needs to behave like they're from the outside. There's a humility that comes with having a beginner's mind; it works for everyone. When you're from the inside, you know how the sausage is made. And that leaves you filled with assumptions, expectations, and biases that can get in the way. Not to mention you might move too quickly because you think you know everything.

The founder needs to believe they have a successor. No founder sets out to cause untold personal and financial stress only to have a fire sale or close the doors. But that can easily happen if the founder doesn't believe they have a proper successor. This essentially traps them, at least mentally. So they stay in the role and they're emotionally tied to it because this is a business they started. They might have taken a second mortgage to support it. They went all in and they created this entity. To say it's like a child isn't an exaggeration because as the first employee at SBI and its Second CEO, I can tell you it's like a fifth child to me to this day. And I wasn't a founder and I'm not even running it on a day-to-day basis anymore.

If you're in a position to counsel a founder on this topic, I highly recommend it. Ego can get in the way, with them thinking no one could possibly do the job well. But if you care about the person and/or the company, it's worth having the conversation.

Finally, some founders are so worried about how someone else will be received that they never get past *I want out!* Remind them about Tim Cook.

Why a Founder Might Want to Exit

Let's rewind to why we're at this critical juncture in the first place: the founder wants out. Understanding a founder's Why informs many decisions that follow, so getting to that Why is integral to what the succession plan looks like and how it's implemented. Here are the most common Whys.

1. *They need to innovate.* Greg has founder DNA, which means he needs to be in an environment that allows for constant innovation. If he's not, he's not happy. And when he's not happy, the people around him aren't happy.

2. *They recognize the business is no longer scaling at the rate it should because they're in the way.* This was also part of what happened at SBI, and it's evident in Kristie's story, as well. What she did to get to a business doing $10 million in revenue wasn't going to be what she needed to do to get to $50 million and she wasn't interested in the latter job. Fortunately, she recognized that and reached out for help.

3. *They're not able to monetize the business.* A typical scenario is a founder who has 90 percent of their net worth tied up in the business; it's great cash flow, but they don't feel like they can monetize it and they feel trapped. This is how most founders of professional services firms feel. They get a few employees,

they start to get some scale, they're making money, and then they realize the business revolves around them. They make the mental leap to *I can't leave. I'm trapped.* They don't see a way out and think they're the exception to every rule, and they're doomed to be stuck there forever.

4. *They get an offer to recap the business or sell a portion of it and maintain their position.* Great news, right? But their response is *If I'm not 100 percent in charge, I don't want to stay here. So I'll take my money, but I'm not gonna stay working for other people.* Founders don't typically like to have a boss or a board.

5. *They wake up one day with a light bulb over their head that says,* "I actually have a successor internally. I love my business, but I think there's somebody better to run it than me, and that person is right under my nose."

6. *There's an offer on the table to buy the business, but the buyers won't take the founder because they know the founder is the problem.* This happens more in product companies than service companies because typically in a service-based business, the founder has a lot of relationships, knows the customers and clients, and the buyers don't want to break that continuity.

The founder's Why isn't something anyone can control. As they say, *it is what it is.* But what everyone does with that information and how they proceed are the actual make-or-break moments. The founder might think wanting to step away is the biggest problem, but it's not. It's information that everyone else needs to be calm and rational about. And there's always a way through if there's a willingness to be reasonable, communicate regularly and honestly, use a tested process to create a plan, and then implement that plan.

The Second Half of My SBI Story

Earlier, I mentioned following Greg was only half of my SBI story. The other half is around my successor, which was similar to taking over for a founder. But that time, I was prepared. My plan was to be out in six years when I was fifty. I had a promise to my wife, Lynne, that when I hit fifty, control of calendar would be at the forefront. We wanted to do other things in our fifties and while being CEO was incredible, you do not have flexibility or optionality in this role. It is all-encompassing. I went in knowing in a few years I should either have an internal person flagged or know I'd be doing an external search. Internal was the case for me because Mike, our COO, was an obvious choice. He was already talented and respected by the employees, and I was grooming him in the service of the scorecard for the next CEO. We had assessed him against the scorecard to find his gaps and got him a coach to address the gaps. It wasn't a guaranteed transition, but the agreement was we'd all do our level best to be honest and open. Mike earned more and more responsibility over about eighteen months and excelled. With about six months left before my exit, I started to signal to the organization that Mike would be taking over. They already knew and loved him, and it went off without a hitch. He's the CEO to this day.

That's the kind of smooth transition that's possible.

Business leadership isn't a marathon; it's a relay race. The first person to hold and pass the baton is the founder, and that person is qualitatively different from the successor CEO. Let's get into why these two creatures are very different, why they're both necessary to successfully scale, and how the baton gets gracefully passed rather than thrown and fumbled. *Hint: whether the handoff is done well is largely based on how you handle it.*

KEY ACCELERANTS

→ Whether you're internal or external, behave as if you're external. That will help neutralize some of the natural bias and subjectivity you have.

→ Your job is about professionalizing the company and scaling. To do that well, you need a management system and a scorecard for your role.

→ Get yourself assessed against the scorecard and find a coach for your gaps.

→ Be the best you that you can be; don't try to replicate the founder's behavior.

→ Don't dive in and make a bunch of changes.

Now let's get you prepared to show up the way you need to as *The Second CEO.*

CAN I REALLY DO THIS?

Yes I Can!

The way the handoff happens is critical to the success of the transition, as you saw in chapter 1. Let's dive deeper into the part of the handoff you can control—how you prepare and show up. Whether you're from the inside or the outside, and whether you're a first-time CEO or not, you're wondering if you're up to the task. You might also be wondering if you'll look back in a year and remember accepting the job as the worst decision of your life. No matter what you're thinking or feeling, this chapter will set you on a course to prioritize what's important and not sweat the small stuff. Sometimes it's tough to tell which is which.

Following a founder is a complex major life transition. I underestimated the importance of what happens in your head, your heart, and your social life when you follow a founder. Even if you've been working with that person for years and the financial bump you get isn't life-altering for you. You're being handed somebody's vision to execute. You're the shepherd of what's usually one of the biggest accomplishments of their life—starting and scaling a business. This is more than a job; following a founder is the biggest responsibility a CEO can have.

My Story, Continued

For the longest time, Greg said he was going to be the CEO forever, so no one was thinking about succession. But the founder DNA I mentioned in chapter 1 eventually dominated, and he wanted to exit. We knew we had the potential to find an investor to help us buy out Greg's shares. This was a very uncertain and emotional time in our partnership. Was the business ready for a full-scale private equity transaction? Or would we go down the path of having an investor help us fund Greg's ownership stake (51 percent) and none of us would take any liquidity? Maybe we would get a deal done, maybe not. This was Greg's deal to make and no one else's; however, there was a lot of emotion wrapped around the partnership (there were six total equity partners of SBI at this time). We had a very close brotherhood, and unfortunately, this process caused some natural separation, not only during the negotiation but also after.

For some reason, it didn't really hit me until the first week of August 2017, when Greg signed the purchase agreement. We would close at the end of August, after three weeks of confirmatory diligence. Now, the investor helping us buy out Greg had already told us they closed 100 percent of their deals, so this was happening.

Meanwhile, I was thinking, *I'm going to be the CEO; this is really going to happen.* I never thought I'd be a CEO; I mean, I never wanted to. Or, if I'm honest with myself, that was just me being intimidated and telling myself I didn't want to be a CEO, because I didn't think I could do it. I was intimidated and nervous. I looked at Greg and other CEOs and I didn't know if I was a visionary. I didn't know if I understood finance the way I needed to or if I could be the creator/ designer of our intellectual property. I was steeped in uncertainty. However, Greg and the partners were beyond supportive of me. They believed in me more than I did, and I'm forever grateful.

I questioned my ability to be a great decision-maker. Greg had this decision-making ability I always relied on. He would quickly, easily validate or invalidate options, and bring amazing clarity to a situation. And all people need clarity to execute well. He had more rights than wrongs when it came to decision-making, so he was doing a lot right.

Greg also had street smarts, and he teaches people how to think differently, which is something I still carry to this day. He knows how to frame a problem and understand what you're solving for. He can think about multiple options at once and not be linear. I wasn't like that at first, so I didn't think I was ready. What I did think was, *I could figure it out alone.*

And I was so wrong about that.

Something else I was wrong about was my initial approach of comparing myself to Greg. Though I think it's perfectly natural and human to do that, resist the temptation as it's not the best use of your bandwidth. You don't want to be a knock-off of the founder; you want to be *the best you* that you can be. I recently spoke with Tom Eggemeier, CEO of Zendesk, following an incredibly successful founder. One of his first tips for Second CEOs was to not spend any time trying to recreate the instincts or behavior of the founder. Tom's advice is spot on and I should have called him eight years ago!

So there I was, with my massive case of impostor syndrome, despite the reality that we'd already been on a multimonth roadshow shopping the firm and had found a very interested investor who wanted to back us in the buyout of Greg's equity. Not only was I chosen by Greg and the partners, but the investors believed in me, too. Clearly, there was outside evidence I was ready. Furthermore, my wife, Lynne, who's been my biggest supporter for almost two decades, didn't blink and thought I was always headed for CEO. She wasn't concerned at all and had unshakable faith in my abilities. The confidence of others meant a lot to me, but it didn't erase the nagging feeling that maybe I couldn't do it.

In retrospect, my impostor syndrome had a very real source: I'd never been a CEO and I didn't have a plan for how I was going to be one. My internal monologue included what I now know are key questions that could have—should have—been answered in the months prior to my first day as CEO:

- As CEO, what do I do differently?

- How do I spend my time?

- What's the definition of a good day?

- What should I focus on from day to day?

I was going to be responsible for things I hadn't had to worry about, and some of them weren't my strengths, but they were Greg's. Marketing and intellectual property, for instance. He couldn't get enough of them. He loved them and was amazing at them, and I don't know where he got his inspiration and I didn't share his enthusiasm for those parts of the job. He molded the CEO position into one that covered marketing and IP, day to day. They were his playground, so that became integral to the CEO position. That's what founders do, and it makes sense. Meanwhile, I don't want to run marketing or intellectual property.

For a while, I did all the things Greg did because I had to; he was gone. Slowly but surely, I figured out what I *shouldn't* be doing, and what a Matt-led SBI should look like compared to what a Greg-led SBI looked like.

What I haven't mentioned is at this point this whole thing was a secret to almost everybody in the firm. For the first month, I kept it under wraps. I did my job as senior partner driving revenue, spent time with Greg learning little bits and pieces, and talked to Aaron, our cofounder and my right hand, about all the things we needed to do for diligence purposes.

All the while, I was thinking:

- *Do I need to wait thirty days before the big reveal?*

- *How do I tell the firm? I've never done anything like this!*

- *What changes am I going to make or do I need to make?* I should have had somebody give us an objective assessment of where the business was and spent time and money addressing whatever changes I needed to make. For example, someone had to do the job I was about to leave vacant. Who would take my place? Two months in, I promoted someone I liked who was already doing a good job in his position but wasn't the best match for the new business leadership role. In my mind, going external carried too much cultural risk. Meanwhile, eighteen months later, I had to change that position. It didn't occur to me at the time, but if I had to do it over again, I would have launched a search right away. I would have looked at outside candidates. And while I may or may not have made an outside hire, identifying competencies the next senior partner should have in order to flourish was a conversation I should have been having. And not just with myself—with some key advisors/mentors I trusted.

- *Do I just slide into the CEO position and everyone else on the team remains the same?* Do I need different people because my strengths are different from Greg's?

On September 1, 2017, Greg and I led an all-hands (every employee) conference call. Greg started the call by sharing he had sold his shares and would be leaving the firm. He shared why and when. It was very brief, and we didn't open the call up for questions. I then spent the back part of the call sharing my enthusiasm, ensuring the team that the journey doesn't stop, and all the customary things the new CEO is supposed to say. The biggest shock to the firm's central nervous system was it was effective immediately. We did the call on a Friday, and on Monday Greg was no longer employed and Matt was CEO. Talk about a shock wave.

The Transition Trifecta

Transitions can have personal, financial, professional, and social consequences. Sometimes they go well by accident, with the person unaware of all the components of the transition and what could have gone wrong. But this is presumably a big moment in your life, and if you've gotten this far in this book, you want all the advice you can get. You want to benefit from the experience of others.

When you're following a founder, you have three transitions to go through, whether or not you realize it.

1. *Your transition out of whatever you were doing.* You might be in a position to craft this moment. The moment this opportunity arises, you should be thinking about how you're going to handle what you currently do.

If you're internal and it's up to you to replace yourself, don't do what I did and pick someone internal you like who's competent and seems like a good fit. That's not thorough enough and will only give *you* a headache somewhere down the line. Instead, make a scorecard for your job and assess people internally for a match. Go external if you don't find one.

    a. What's your mindset about leaving your current position? What are relationships like? Are there job-related projects to complete or hand off? What's the most professional way to leave that creates the smallest wake possible and paves a clear, smooth path for whoever comes after you?

    b. Leave well. Whether you've been at a company for years or not, be certain to put as much attention, intention, and integrity into exiting as you will to moving into your new position.

2. *Your transition into CEO.* It's easy to overlook having a plan when you're internal. After all, you know the person, you've seen them work, you likely know the KPIs and benchmarks, and you think you know the job. Though that might seem intuitive, it's far from reality. Everyone needs a plan. And watching someone do something is different from doing it yourself. Chapter 4 will detail what to do in the days, weeks, and months. For now, know that there are two equally important aspects of the job: business and personal.

    a. Whatever happened in the past, it's far more important than it used to be to be a CEO people want to work for. What kind of culture do you want to create? What kind of leader do you want to be? If you're internal, how are you going to handle the relationships with coworkers now that you're "the boss?" I got along with everyone well, but I definitely felt a shift in the way people spoke to me once I was CEO. There's a natural tendency for people to change their tone and approach when the CEO shows up on a call. And it's your job to be as disarming as possible. You don't need an inauthentic environment where people want to be on their best behavior. You're just another team member with different responsibilities. I didn't quite get that at first, and I felt like a fish out of water; I wasn't sure who I was supposed to be.

I've always been someone with a huge capacity for work who loves working. I also had been an owner in the firm since 2011, and as we built equity value through the firm's growth, my equity appreciated. Unfortunately, we didn't have a plan that allowed all employees to participate in this growth. So in the beginning, I managed people as if they had that same capacity for and love of work. I was wrong. This is classic founder behavior. And while I was not a founder of SBI, as the first employee I leaned much more to founder ethos than that of a professional, tenured CEO.

And so if I was on an email, I'd weigh in. I'd want to weigh in on everything. In my head, everything was a priority for me. I had no idea what a good day or a good week looked like. The team wanted clear direction and I couldn't give it to them. I was just reacting to my emails and to my calendar, not owning my time and establishing priorities.

Out of fear or lack of confidence, I started acting like a dictator rather than giving myself time to determine who I wanted to be as a leader. I had always had a strong, commanding temperament, but one thing I didn't realize is that in this role, trying to drive everything as a sales leader isn't effective. CEOs must be able to enable people to bring their best selves to work. Through this inspiration, employees do their best. I fractured some relationships early because it was like I was performing. I wasn't being Matt; I was acting like a leader I thought would get things done. It took a while to learn to show some vulnerability and settle into being me. No one is all things. We all make mistakes, we all have strengths, and working together is the only way to move forward.

Unfortunately, it took a wake-up call of having to lay off 10 percent of the firm for me to realize I wasn't aware of our indicators. When you have a major investor, you need good management hygiene, including an actual management method for running and scaling the business.

b. This brings me to values. Your values as an individual might change, your family's values might change, and the firm's values might need to be revised. As a company, we changed our core values, our purpose, and our vision. And our strategy for cascading those values throughout the firm involved leaning on more senior people to take the lead on that.

c. Be on the lookout for things to change for you socially. Your friends from back in the day won't care much about your new position because they love you for who you are deep down. But in reality, you have a new peer group. New people come out of the woodwork when you become CEO. You'll be invited to exclusive events, you'll be contacted by nonprofits, and other CEOs will reach out for a variety of reasons. Don't let your new status distract you. Those people aren't going anywhere and will continue to check in with you. It might feel good and make you feel important, but don't allow yourself to get distracted by all the new attention.

d. Pay attention to your habits of well-being. Celebrate if that's your style, but then get to work. Transitions take mental, emotional, and even physical energy, and you can easily get run down after the initial adrenaline and dopamine wear off. If you don't have good sleep hygiene, get on that, as there are very few people who can function optimally when they are under-slept. Even though I have solid habits around sleep, attached to Greg leaving was we had a debt payment due every month, and I felt this massive amount of pressure that negatively affected my sleep. For the first year, I would wake up at 2:00 a.m. with thirty-seven things on my mind. *I gotta do this. I got to do that.* It was awful. You have to have something you do to decompress and center yourself, otherwise it can be really tough on your mind and body. I was always on, from day one, and that took its toll. I couldn't turn off the thoughts swirling about expectations, revenue, and the debt payments.

3. *Your transition into the team.* Depending on the size of the company, the leadership team might have four to eight other people on it. I've seen newly minted CEOs focus on swapping out every single person immediately, and I've seen them not prioritize that for good reasons. The reason for the immediate swap is: *Why waste time getting into a groove with people who aren't **your** people?* Swapping out immediately is efficient, as you don't have to get used to one team, and then another. Furthermore, starting with a clean slate prevents gossip carryover from the founder's tenure, which can be toxic and time-wasting. For now, know that if the leadership team is going to be there for a while, integrating a new person takes time and energy. Relationships don't always magically settle into a healthy groove; they take time and attention.

I was in a delicate position because I had two cofounders, Mike and Aaron, who each owned more of the business than I did and had been there longer than I had, but I was the CEO. There was tension that sometimes escalated and was pretty uncomfortable. We had to make a shift with one of the cofounders and change his role. Initially he wasn't happy about that, but there was respect for my decisions. And his self-awareness and love for the firm allowed this change to happen smoothly. The dynamic mellowed with time, and we are the best of friends now, with so much in the rearview mirror.

Setting Yourself Up for a Successful Transition Trifecta

There are three steps you can take to set yourself up for a successful transition trifecta: (1) have the right mindset; (2) create an informal board for yourself; and (3) develop a scorecard.

A curious, compassionate, adventurous mindset will take you a long way as you start your new chapter. You should have *curiosity* in spades. There's nothing worse than coming into a new position thinking you already know everything. Remember that your worthiness has already been established because you got the job. What you have to demonstrate now is a willingness to have what's known as *beginner's mind*—to have enough confidence to be a learner.

This is also where *empathy* comes in. You're presumably surrounded by people whose positions have *not* changed the way yours has. But your presence as CEO is new to them. So in a way, their positions *have* changed, because they involve getting to know how you work and communicate—how you relate—as a CEO. That takes a period of adjustment for all of you, and a mindset of generosity and kindness will set a foundation for a smooth transition for all of you.

To round out your mindset, I'll end with *adventurous*. When you add *explorer* to your identity in addition to CEO, you're less likely to fall into acting the way you think you should act. Allow yourself time to observe. Don't jump in and start doing, changing, commanding. Explore doing things differently, but only after careful observation and assessment. Don't permanently change anything or make irreversible decisions in the first days and weeks.

To help you determine what decisions you really do need to make, like swapping out the leadership team, for instance, it's best to have a small informal board of mentors. I recommend three people who each contribute a different perspective, who know you fairly well, and who aren't *Yes Men*. These are people with a common goal of helping you make the best decisions, be aware of your blind spots, coach you through conflict, and build you up when you need it.

Your board might feel strongly about you replacing key people first thing. They should be so trustworthy, experienced, and skilled at communicating that you understand why and they can even suggest the best way to have the conversation. For this kind of relationship to work, you have to be open, vulnerable, and honest. And you have to be receptive to other ways of thinking and doing.

Finally, if you don't have a scorecard for the CEO position where you're the CEO, you need to make one. And here's where your leadership team will be vital. The founder's team as well as their scorecard—if there is one—is likely based on what the founder did as CEO. This is different from what *you* as the CEO will be doing. The founder's leadership team was likely assembled to compensate for that person's weaknesses and to cover the areas they weren't enthusiastic about. Do you see why the first act of a new CEO is often to replace the leadership team? And do you see why a fresh scorecard might be in order, even if there is one?

Why Founders Don't Usually Have Scorecards

AND WHY SCORECARDS ARE CRUCIAL FOR CEOS

Most founders don't have scorecards. What they usually do have is a description of what they do that needs to be done. That list is composed of things they probably *should* be doing as well as things they've come to do or they like to do but they *shouldn't* be doing.

Here's how that typically happens. In the early stages, the founder and CEO is one person. So you have a visionary—an idea person with an unwavering belief in their mission—sometimes doing everything. They're changing the world, one industry, one service, one product at a time. At the same time, they're patching together sales funnels, websites, social media, email campaigns, thought leadership, distribution, and even manufacturing and shipping. Maybe there's a cofounder who's the technical person and makes the visionary's idea into a reality. Either way, you have a fast-paced environment with too few people and not enough resources to get everything done, plus "everything" hasn't necessarily been well-defined.

Founders tend to be risk-takers, unbothered by convention or bureaucracy. They propel the company forward and are usually the face of it, creating emotional connections with customers who become evangelists of the brand. All of this is a recipe for two things, for sure:

1. The founder is doing at least a few things they shouldn't be doing because those things aren't a good use of their time, they're not particularly good at them, or they don't enjoy them. But at the beginning, those things need to get done, so founders will figure it out. They won't necessarily do things the best, fastest, smartest, or least expensive way, but they *will* get them done.

2. Being idea people, founders can easily fall into a lack of focus, overlook operational details, and/or change things because they're bored. They can also fail to see that something (or someone) isn't working out because they don't have defined metrics. They might even get used to mediocrity. This creates chaos as the company scales.

While the founder is driven by passion and purpose, the CEO is driven by execution and results. This is the yin to the founder's yang, the pragmatist tasked with converting lofty ambitions into a well-oiled machine.

Unlike the founder, the CEO must strike a delicate balance between creativity and structure. CEOs are process people who bring discipline to the organization, implementing systems that optimize efficiency. CEOs are adept at navigating complex landscapes, making tough decisions, and mitigating risks. They are the captains, responsible for managing resources, attracting investment, and ensuring profitability.

The CEO's power lies in their ability to assemble and lead a high-performing team. They recruit talent and foster a culture of innovation and accountability. A CEO's success hinges on their ability to inspire trust and unite individuals toward a common goal. They are the conductors of a symphony, orchestrating the collective talents of their employees, who each play their part to perfection. They professionalize what the founder started.

In some cases, founders transition into the role of CEO, leveraging their deep understanding of the company's DNA. This ensures the preservation of the founder's vision while benefiting from the CEO's operational expertise. What's more common is a founder recognizing they're not a CEO, which is a necessary first step toward securing one and is a good sign.

A less-good sign is a founder who doesn't believe anyone can do the job except them, and they stagnate. Often for years. This founder might pour their life and savings into the business, take out a second mortgage, and become wildly over-leveraged. They're sure the next change to their product or service, or the next rockstar hire, is going to launch them. They don't realize they've shackled themselves to the notion that there's no one out there who can do their company justice. Either they never set out to identify a CEO, or they do it in a half-hearted way that fails and confirms there's no one out there for the job.

If you've been identified as the person to follow the founder, your founder's vision has allowed them to see that their company—their baby—needs a different kind of leadership than what they can offer. This is great news for you, because even if your founder needed to be nudged by the board or an advisor to step back, they're willing to. That's forward movement. And the best way to maintain or boost your momentum is to create a scorecard for your new job.

Your Identity

WHO ARE YOU AS A CEO?

Whoever you're following, they made a mark. On people and on culture—in hearts and minds. That mark might be profound in a *tough-act-to-follow* kind of way, and it also might be profound in a *these-people-are-wounded-and-there's-healing-that-needs-to-happen* kind of way. The next two chapters will dive into this, but for now, ask yourself who you want to be as a CEO, whether or not this is your first time. What does this company need, and how can you best provide it?

Now, you might not know what the company needs, particularly if you don't have a scorecard yet. For example, you might not know if your resources are being directed toward the biggest priorities because you might not know what those priorities are. Remember that few founders ever had a scorecard. By definition, it's not how they operate as they're in the business of figuring out what the product or service is, how best to package it, who the ideal customer is, and how they should price. They're fluid and constantly changing, and that's possible because they're lean and nimble as an organization. Sometimes the priorities of the founder change and the resources of all kinds—people, money, tech—change with the priorities. Sometimes they make that clear to everyone, and sometimes they don't.

Whether or not you think of it this way, this is a style of leadership, and it creates a particular culture marked by uncertainty and confusion. And that inevitably leads to resentment, anger, and turnover. Sometimes when you're internal and you've been subject to a certain style, you try to duplicate it when you take over. Meanwhile, it's not like it worked for the founder, and you can personally attest to it! You have to decide who you want to be as a leader, and though you might not have all the details worked out, making the scorecard a priority is making a statement about your leadership. It's telling everyone that clarity is a big part of who you are as a leader. That clarity begins with you and your own clarity in the form of your scorecard.

KEY ACCELERANTS

→ Whether or not you think you're ready, remember that if you were chosen for this position, other people are convinced you're the person for the job.

→ This is a major life transition, and you should prepare yourself for possible social, personal, emotional, and financial effects. Make sure you have solid habits for well-being and for meeting the many stressors likely to show up.

→ There are three things going on: your transition out of wherever you were/are, your transition into the position, and your transition into the team. It's not unusual to imme-diately swap out your executive team with your own people.

→ Your job as CEO is to professionalize and scale. The way you function is different from the way the founder func-tioned. Don't try to be like them. Be the best version of you, doing the job of CEO.

Chapter 4 will get into the details of exactly what you should be doing and thinking about in your first days, weeks, and months as CEO. Before we get to the nuts and bolts of the job, let's examine what could be the most difficult part of this entire endeavor: working with the founder.

WORKING WITH
THE FOUNDER

Case Study—INSIGHT2PROFIT

In 2006, Ryan White started INSIGHT2PROFIT, a company that specializes in the implementation and optimization of pricing strategies. From then until 2020, he was the face of the firm. Ryan knew everything about everything, and he was very prominent in business development. He decided to step away after almost fifteen years, and he was clear about what he wanted in the CEO who would follow him.

Ryan is a person with high standards. He expected the person who would take over for him to be of the same ilk. He decided to hire a search firm to support the search for his replacement. The first search firm he worked with told him the person he was looking for didn't exist. He didn't believe that. He realized the search would take time and he didn't want to settle. He had a keen sense of self-awareness. In his case, he knew it would take time for him to give up control and that it would be best if he did it over time.

Trust and respect are Ryan's top nonnegotiables. He has to trust and respect you, and he makes those decisions fairly quickly. Running and growing INSIGHT2PROFIT was complex and multifaceted. He wanted to feel comfortable handing off and backing away from the firm, one part at a time. The best way to do that, in his mind, was to have an interim executive come on as president. And the best way to do that was to choose someone he already knew, trusted, and respected.

Erasmo Schutzer volunteered to facilitate Ryan's transition and assume the role of president. Erasmo was on the board and was a client for six years. He and Ryan had mutual respect and were aligned on personal values, which was important for both of them. Erasmo's goal was to demonstrate the company could be successfully run by someone other than the founder. He admired Ryan's leadership skills as well as the ability of the company to execute. Finally, Erasmo had nothing to lose as he was pondering retirement. The prospect of helping Ryan transition out was interesting to him personally and professionally, and he wanted the best for Ryan and his company.

The skill and wisdom of Ryan's strategy deserves to be unpacked in more detail:

- *Ryan knew it was time to step away because he was no longer enjoying running the company.* I've coached founders as well as those following founders. There are plenty of founders who don't recognize when it's time for them to step away. On the other hand, there are founders who are fully aware that they shouldn't still be running their company, and they don't even want to anymore. But they're entirely convinced that no one can fill their shoes. Kudos to Ryan for knowing it was time.

- *Ryan knew the transition to someone new would take time.* Kudos, again, for not listening to the original firm. Ryan knew that though no one else would have the same connection to the company that he had, there were plenty of talented, trustworthy people out there who could run it well. He only had to find one of them.

- *Going the route of president/interim CEO addressed Ryan's biggest perceived challenges.* He already had someone he trusted in Erasmo. Having him assume the role of president bought Ryan time, which he knew he might need.

- *Handing off projects, departments, and clients to Erasmo was easier than doing so with a stranger.* And once Ryan was out of something, he was out. It would be up to Erasmo to hand everything off to whomever the search identified.

Erasmo's tenure was supposed to be six to eight months, but ended up being more than twice that. During that time, he grew the business at a rate of over 20 percent. Let's look at his takeaways.

Erasmo's Major Takeaways

When Erasmo came on as president, he and Ryan thought they would be able to tell after three or four months if it was the right fit. And they were correct. In that time, Ryan was increasingly comfortable that Erasmo could run the business and wouldn't change strategy. Erasmo knew that the key to this working was Ryan had to feel like Erasmo could work with his journey from micromanaging to making an effort to move on.

Erasmo didn't have some kind of *Am I ready?* moment in the way I did. His moment was more like, *Is this going to work?* And that's because unlike me, he'd be working alongside the founder for months, which is more customary than just taking over one day, like I did. As Erasmo says, "The question you have to ask yourself is: Am I willing to work with the founder during the many times I will have to step back and adjust to the founder's journey for the sake of the big picture? Do I know when to lose a certain battle for the sake of the bigger war?"

Part of the founder's journey is also: Is the founder ready to have the company led in a different way? Successful founders have succeeded, in their minds, because they've done things a certain way. Because of that, they tend to think the way they did it is the best way. If you're considering a position following a founder, explore whether that person thinks anyone else has good ideas. There's a lot of risk with someone who thinks they're always right, especially if they're analytical and data-driven and in fact are right much of the time. But being right doesn't mean there aren't other ways to succeed, and those ways could reflect a leadership style that has a higher probability of success for the company.

Because the founder's journey underpins the entire experience for both the founder and their successor, it behooves the successor to get to know the founder as deeply as possible. This includes their personality, values, approach to solving problems, beliefs, clarity on strategy, and decision-making style. Interview the leadership team, too. Try to understand the founder's personal, professional, and financial backstory. Insight into the founder helps you understand how ready and motivated they are to move on. As Erasmo says, "You want to minimize the possibility that they will have buyer's remorse. There are leading indicators that the founder will have buyer's remorse."

Here are some questions you definitely want the answers to, according to Erasmo:

- What's the founder's next project? What are they going to do when all that time becomes available? We know they intend to move *away* from something, but are they also moving *toward* something?

- What do they want to know on a monthly or quarterly basis? Ask. If they always want an excruciating level of detail, that's a leading indicator of possible buyer's remorse.

- How often do they want to meet? Does the founder have a transition plan, and what are the milestones nearing the end? What does the transition plan look like? We outlined each area of responsibility and the transition to me.

INSIGHT2PROFIT found their permanent CEO in Carl Will, a veteran of following founders. He followed Erasmo and has been the CEO since February of 2022. Carl has accelerated the growth of INSIGHT2PROFIT at a rate three times the consulting growth rate average. Complete home run.

Erasmo took what was successful from his transition with Ryan to his handoff to Carl Will. It took eighteen months to find Carl, partially because this was during COVID, and partially because the office is in Ohio and presence in the office, with the team, was non-negotiable. But that patience paid off. Carl had the right leadership skills, personality, and emotional intelligence and was clearly the right person for the job. As Erasmo said, "We were all convinced about Carl; it was total consensus."

Carl's Major Takeaways

This is Carl's third time following a founder, and he loves it. He loves "the possibility to write some new chapters that are a little different and still preserve all the goodness of the founder and their fingerprints all over the business." Carl's transition went well, and both he and Erasmo enjoyed it. Like Erasmo, Carl recommends clarity with the founder (or president, as in this case) regarding their presence and engagement.

Carl spoke at length about the skill with which Erasmo handled his interim position. "They [Erasmo and Ryan] shared so much. Board presentations, working-session notes, visions … they had an intensive inner process. … And another plus was they were very open to some things being different."

Both Erasmo and Carl spoke about a common interpersonal issue when working with a founder, which is the fact that *this is their baby, and part of your job is to help them let go.* Carl recalls saying to Ryan, "Do you think you can be the kind of owner I can call with a problem, and you won't have a billion neurons firing in your brain and a strong desire to jump in? At some point you have to be that kind of board member. Otherwise, the gravitational pull is too big."

What's Carl's advice for Second CEOs?

- Be yourself.

- Respect who the founder is and celebrate what they've done, and then take advantage of what they know and how they can help you create something different that's equally amazing.

- Give the founder opportunities to engage in ways that help you help them. If you have a healthy founder with good intentions, that goes a long way to making your job easier and more enjoyable.

- Don't have an ego. *Your power source is that the founder made you the CEO.* It's not a competition; it's a partnership.

- Nobody's perfect and no situation is without its challenges or even annoyances. *Take the good and leave the rest—leave the bad.* If someone is usually right but their delivery gets under your skin, leave the delivery and recognize that their instincts or thinking is good. If someone has a big ego but they also have high integrity, take the integrity.

As discussed previously, when you're internal and the founder is sticking around, whether for the long term or for a transition period, there's a tendency to want to lead like that person. I think it's natural. I did it, and plenty of situations I've been brought into had that dynamic. You've been watching this person operate for years, and clearly they were successful by some metrics; otherwise they would be completely gone already and the business wouldn't have gone as far as it has. Even if the founder's behavior was toxic and abusive, and everyone knows it including the person following the founder, that doesn't necessarily prevent the same behavior in the new CEO.

I'm not a therapist, but this could be a case of humans repeating what they know without taking the time to reflect and assess their own experience. It's also a reality that humans tend to act out in a bad way when they're not confident, not clear, under-slept, and over-caffeinated. Remember the habits I discussed earlier? This is where you reap the benefits of taking care of your mind and body. When your mind is clear and you're calm and grounded, you're a lot less likely to develop destructive interpersonal habits.

There's also the mistake of feeling like there are cultural and operating norms that the founder started that are therefore gospel to the business so you can't alter them. You've seen that there are components tied to the identity of the company and you don't even consider touching them. But I'm here to tell you that you can adjust how to run the executive team and what that looks like.

For example, at SBI, Greg had started an annual summer camp for kids nine to eighteen. It was a wonderful event each summer and personified Greg. This allowed Greg an opportunity to teach SBI kids some life skills, make memories, and bring the firm closer together. When I took over, we decided to eliminate this—not because it wasn't a great tradition but because the firm was evolving. We were starting to have more younger employees, and as a virtual firm, we needed to focus on more in-person get-togethers to build culture. Many of the younger employees were feeling left out, and there were enough complaints, so we shifted to doing regional midyear events to bring employees together. Greg and I had similar objectives—drive employee engagement—but we chose to execute on that objective in different ways.

The scorecard is essential here in that it keeps you focused on what's important and helps you explain the way things are going to go moving forward. If culture is problematic, part of your scorecard, by definition, will be cultivating a culture of safety, openness, excellence, fun, or whatever has come out of the scorecard-creation process. If you follow your scorecard, not only won't you thrash around in your new job while being simultaneously frustrated that you can't get out of your old job, but you'll also pay attention to culture. Your scorecard keeps you moving forward with clarity. When you feel good about what you're doing and you're on track, it's easier to reengage with key employees who may have been alienated by the founder's behavior.

Invaluable Advice from a Founder-CEO

David DeWolf founded and scaled 3 Pillar Global, a Product-Development-as-a-Service (PDaaS) firm, at an amazing rate and was its CEO for more than sixteen years. The insight he has from his vantage point is invaluable. He happens to have buckets of self-awareness, which is evident in his advice. Here are his most compelling observations, as a long-time founder and CEO who eventually tossed the baton, and who's been exploring potential next opportunities.

- When you're in a high-growth business, the brutal reality is you have to reinvent yourself about every eighteen months. The job changes over and over again, and some people love that challenge and can navigate it and play all those different altitudes. Others don't find that fun and prefer one phase of the journey. Know that's coming your way.

- For any CEO, the secret to knowing when to step away is what I call *humble competence*—having the ability to listen and really digest the advice of your mentors and others, but also being confident in who you are and knowing what your skills are. Mentors are crucial, as are board members. We all have blind spots and being a good listener while being discerning is important.

- Most of the time, the founder doesn't give the new operator enough space. And when that happens, there's confusion about who's in charge. The number one thing is for the founder to truly commit to stepping back and allowing the new CEO to step in. They should be available and not just walk away. They should have a healthy distance from the business while still supporting it. Someone shouldn't even accept the position until they've set up the dynamic in a healthy way. Ask about their involvement and what they like doing or still want to do. Get a feel for how likely they are to be able to do whatever they said they would do—walk away, transition over ninety days or six months or whatever.

- Since I transitioned out and there's a new CEO in place, I've had several different businesses ask me if I'd want to be their CEO. I've looked at those different options, and I'm paying attention to how they're going to transition. I won't just interview with the private equity fund and the board and then be placed in there. I want to know, How is the current CEO or founder thinking about this? What's their perspective on their role moving forward? What's this going to look like? What's the plan? How do we have a healthy working relationship from the get-go? If you want to be set up for success, I think everybody in that situation has to have those radically candid hard conversations up front and set boundaries and set up the situation to be healthy.

- If a founder is too addicted to certain things and unwilling to let go, that's a red flag. Sometimes there's another party who wants a new CEO and the founder really isn't looking for one. When you speak with the founder early on, it's very much like interviewing for a job. It doesn't really matter what they say; it's what they really believe that's important. And to figure that out, you have to have the emotional intelligence to read the body language and facial expressions and to get to what they really believe.

- You're going to come with your own perspective. You don't want the founder to just agree with you. What you want them to do is tell you how it's going to work from their perspective and how they're going to bring your two worlds together.

Do These Four Things

It's rare that a founder just leaves and is gone forever, as in my story. They usually keep a role on the board, at least. Before you start crafting your identity as CEO and deciding how and when you'll do things differently, you need to do four things:

1. *Get input from the executive team and key employees.* You want their opinions. You want to benefit from their experiences. You want to know what the CEO of this business should stop doing and what they should keep doing. Not what should Matt do, *what should the CEO of this business do?* This isn't personal, and I could be anyone. Simple, informal feedback is what you want. And once you have it, you start to triangulate. If you hear something once, you can dismiss it. But if you hear it two or three times, you have a legitimate data point and you're onto something you'll likely need to act on. Chapter 4 has much more on this.

2. *Define the scorecard.* Ask, If I have a great first year as incoming CEO, what do you, the founder and a large shareholder, think that looks like? Document their thoughts, and after the first ninety days, see what you were right about and wrong about.

3. *Be patient and empathetic.* The organization is having to learn how to operate without the founder, and they're going to have trust issues. They'll be wondering whether they like you, whether they trust you, and whether you're competent. They're in wait-and-see mode, judging what you do and don't do. That's OK, and they need to know that.

They also need your patience. They're likely to ask a lot of questions about why you're doing what you're doing, and you might find yourself having to explain more than you want to. And the moment you think you're done communicating a message as CEO, you'll find you need to say it again. You're never done. Know that now, and be patient.

4. *Celebrate your small wins.* Connecting with people in the first ninety days? Win! Having one-to-one conversations up and down the organization? Win! Getting feedback from small focus groups about what they think you should start doing or stop doing? Win!

Greg's New Firm and What You Can Learn from It

When Greg left SBI, he took a couple of years off to decompress. From traveling to golf to taking a few classes, he entered a wandering period. Many refer to this as "halftime"—the time between the first half of your life and setting up the second half. There's a wonderful book by Bob Buford called *Halftime—Moving from Success to Significance*, which I highly recommend. Greg founded Collective 54 three years later, which is the first mastermind community for boutique professional services firms. It's a community of founders who want to grow, scale, and sell their boutiques. Collective 54 has identified five effective leadership styles.[1]

This list is helpful for getting insight into the founder you're following as well as figuring out what kind of leader you want to be.

---

1   Collective 54 and Greg Alexander, "The 5 leadership styles of the most successful founders of professional service firms...and the one to avoid," Collective 54, October 2, 2022, accessed September 24, 2023, https://www.collective54.com/blogs/the-5-leadership-styles-of-the-most-successful-founders-of-professional-service-firmsand-the-one-to-avoid/.

1. THE CAPABILITY SEDUCER

These founders look for expertise everywhere. They ignore conventional practices like CVs, degrees, job histories, etc. They find trapped and hidden genius in the most unlikely places. And they have an almost sixth sense in spotting a person's native capability (e.g., something they do exceptionally well and easily that is in high demand). Often, these individuals are unaware that what they are good at is in high demand. Thus, the Capability Seducer becomes a matchmaker, connecting the hidden talent with the opportunity.

2. THE EMANCIPATOR

The Emancipator frees employees from the soul-crushing work environment of big corporate America, where they exist under constant restraints. These employees are capable of so much more than their jobs in corporate America allow them to contribute, and the Emancipator knows it.

An Emancipator creates elbow room for their employees to thrive. This is not done by accident. It is deliberate. It shows up most often in the work assignment process. Emancipators build slack into each project and encourage employees to lean into it and contribute.

Most compelling of all the traits of the Emancipator leadership style is that they fail often, early, cheap, and fast. It is because of this that they rapidly move along the learning curve and out-hustle their competitors.

3. THE DEFIER

The Defier constantly tests and stretches their employees. They believe people grow by being challenged and that firms grow by never being content. They're often heard saying, "Grow through what you are going through." Their teaching style is Socratic, never providing the answer but rather just the provocative question, allowing the employee to discover the answer on their own.

The Defier does two things over and over again. First, they lay down a huge "stretch challenge" and make it concrete, tangible, and measurable. They assign ownership of the challenge to their high-potential employees, allowing them to be in the hot seat.

Secondly, they generate a belief in their high-potential employees that the impossible is possible. The stretch assignment has a plan, timeline, deliverables, milestones, a budget, and resources. The Defier sends the message: "I defy you to pull this off."

4. THE HEAD BUMPER

The Head Bumper believes any problem can be solved if enough heads are put on it, that is, "Let's bump heads on this." They like to argue point/counterpoint style. Working for the Head Bumper can feel like working in a courtroom whereby two sides argue an issue with a judge handling procedure and a jury issuing a verdict. This style of leader believes that no one has all the answers.

The Head Bumper makes ten decisions before most of us have had our first cup of coffee and runs a fast firm. This is because the Head Bumper is a fast framer. They quickly frame up the decision to be made, the options to choose from, whose input is needed, and how the decision shall be made (as in by majority, consensus, etc.). The Head Bumper sparks a robust debate and calls on everyone to provide input. They delete opinions and listen only to facts. They overweight input from those most educated on a topic. And they have an uncanny knack for balancing rigor and creating a safe place to bang heads.

This leader doesn't care who won or lost the argument, only that a sound decision was made.

5. THE SPONSOR

The sponsor is the opposite of a micromanager and is as hands-off as one can possibly be. They sponsor a project or an executive, and they empty the bank account in support of the initiative. They name a lead and make sure everyone knows that the success or failure of the initiative sits with this lead. They stretch this person, hold the lead accountable, and do not care how the objective is accomplished, only that it is.

To become a sponsor, you need to be bold and bet big. Sponsors step in only when the person on the hook needs knowledge and resources to deliver. They teach and coach but never "do." They also expect a complete job and reject partial work, demanding only solutions and not more new problems. Ultimately, Sponsors allow people to experience the natural consequences of their actions.

Finally, there's the leadership style to avoid: It's called the *Pleaser*. The Pleaser has the best of intentions. They think they're doing a good job but are not and just do not know any better.

If the founder was a Pleaser, odds are you'll see the consequences of that when you speak with your employees and hear about culture. If your Pleaser will be around for a significant period of time during your transition, it will be critical for you to tightly define a role for them. You're likely going to need to help them recognize that in this role, they're not "the former CEO." They're an employee and they provide something of value that you, the CEO, believes the business needs. This is absolutely essential to ensure the employees don't get confused about who is leading the company.

KEY ACCELERANTS

→ Understanding the founder and being sensitive to their journey is crucial. You must respect the past and what has gotten the company to where it is. Though the founder is embedded in the story of the company, it's time to turn the page and start a new chapter. The way you communicate around the past and moving forward is important, and it sets the tone. This isn't a topic that can handle a lot of feather-ruffling, so the utmost respect in messaging is paramount.

→ Ascertain how the founder wants to communicate and when, and what they need in order to be able to step away, even if it's piecemeal. Create a system they're comfortable with.

→ Identify their style of leadership, and don't try to duplicate it unless it's your style.

→ Know what your style is and that you can change it with coaching and practice.

→ Listen carefully to the founder to get their perspective on how they think your two worlds will meet.

Now that you're set up mentally for what's to come, let's get into the nuts and bolts of what you'll be doing in the first ninety days.

AM I DOING IT RIGHT?

The First Days, Weeks, and Quarter

This chapter and chapter 5 will detail what you should be thinking about and doing by the end of your first six months. From deciding whether to accept the position to mapping out your strategy, I'll take you through it step by step, including samples of cornerstones of your business culture such as purpose, vision, and values.

Overview of the First Ninety Days

The first ninety days are about getting a sense of the current state by talking to customers and employees, understanding the market, and validating what you built in your thesis in the interview process. Here's a balcony view of what you'll think about and do.

- Do you want the job? Pre-acceptance discovery (may or may not apply to you).

- Take a beat to process this life transition.

- Identify a coach or mentor.

- Speak with other CEOs about the position.

- Listening Tour—speaking with your key people internally for all of the Whats, Whys, Hows, and Whens of their positions. You want to know what the company should start doing, stop doing, and keep doing. You're also looking for their perception of the purpose, vision, and values of the firm. These last three will be discussed, in depth, in the next chapter.

- Present your findings to the firm.

If you're interviewing for a role to follow a founder in a dynamic company, you first want to know how to determine if you want the job. Ideally, this involves plenty of time with the founder to discuss the history of the company and what they think it can become. This can be a delicate series of conversations, depending on how and why the founder is stepping down as CEO. Maybe they're getting nudged out by the board, maybe they're bored and ready for their next thing, and maybe there's all kinds of anger and resentment about the founder and you're wary. Frequently, the founder is leaving because they realize they don't have the skill set or desire to take the business to the next level.

Whatever the reason, your job is one of compassion for their journey and understanding enough about what they think the business can become so you can determine if successor to this particular founder is a job you want. If it is, being on board with their vision is important, as much of your work will be about activating and even augmenting that vision.

You also need to speak with the board to get a sense of how hands-on they are and whether there are any restrictions for the CEO. For example, the CEO should always have veto power for who is on the board. You need total accountability for your team, and that includes the board.

This can be a point of contention with some private equity investors. I've met many great investors who've been world class at generating returns for their constituents. They always say "We are investors, not operators so let's not confuse our roles." If that's the case, they shouldn't have a problem with you building a board that's always adding value. And the only way you know for sure that they will allow that is to ask before you accept the offer. From the start, when working with your lead investor, you want to collaborate on what the ideal board for the company would look like. And you want that conversation to center on, *How can we ensure we build a board that will help the executive team accomplish their objectives with more certainty?*

If you hear all the right answers and you do want the job, you want to transition seamlessly, and I'll get into how that happens. Lastly, you want a road map for putting your own authentic footprint on the business while respecting the founder's vision and continuing to create value.

Recall there's your transition into the role as an individual, and there's also what you need in a team, which might be different from what the founder needed. Both of those need to be well-planned and executed. If you're internal, you also need to consider the transition from whatever position you were in into CEO and how you'll handle the gap you're leaving.

Something many internal people have a tough time with is their own lack of objectivity about the role, the people, the history, and the culture. All that is in their head making noise, and being able to separate the signals from that noise and focus on what's really important—even recognizing what's important—isn't easy.

At this early moment, you'll wish you had a coach or mentor. This is the time to identify someone who's objective and clear-thinking, and preferably experienced at making good decisions with incomplete information. Maybe there's a board member or a peer who can help you and be your accountability person. Also contact one or two other CEOs you know and ask them for objective feedback on the role. Is it an extra benefit if they are in an adjacent industry/business model? Sure. But their industry and company size don't matter as much because there are always overlaps in what they do. CEOs, regardless of company size, are in one business: the people business. A good CEO will provide you with what you need most: high-quality questions you'll have to answer. And while you're doing that, you're getting to know the company and defining the role.

Your First Days

Congratulations on the new job! Here are the three things you need to do immediately.

1. *Write a letter to your future self.* Congratulate yourself for getting to the top of the hill and express some gratitude for how blessed you are for this opportunity. Spend time writing about how you feel and what you want to get done in your first year. Then put it away and take it out in ninety days to review it and refine it. Documenting your thoughts and assumptions and then going back to reread them is a powerful exercise for checking in with yourself and your state of mind.

2. *Announce your Listening Tour.* Communication and transparency are crucial early on, as you're establishing trust. People

won't follow someone they don't trust. Everyone needs to know you have a plan for the first year, and what that plan is.

This is all about discovery. Tell your people you'll be speaking to everyone, and that includes the competition and getting a real sense of them. You're going to have structured conversations with each functional leader and present what you've learned. You care about what they have to say and how they feel. You want 100 percent transparency about what you're doing, how much time you've allotted (the first ninety days), and what's going to happen with their input and the wisdom they've accumulated. They need to know you've heard them.

They also need to know how important values are to you. Values aren't some add-on; they're integral to the operation of the company and the creation of its culture. Values define how you behave as a company. The following chapter will go deeper into values.

During your internal Listening Tour, you should be asking five questions for every statement you make. Keep that 5:1 ratio in mind to prevent yourself from thinking you know more than you do. It's too early to claim expertise about anything. You'll ask a lot of Why questions, and that's as it should be. When it comes to operations, there will be a lot of How questions, too. You're effectively acting like a tourist in a foreign country. At the end of ninety days, you know the food, the language, the public transportation, and the taxes. You know what it means to live there. You know the values and the culture. And you didn't know that ninety days ago.

Even if you're internal, don't assume you know what each person actually does to drive shareholder value or what they think about the company's values. Discuss the purpose and vision. Ask questions and just listen. And get into the weeds. Learn exactly what everyone thinks their place is and how they demonstrate the company's values, ask about each line of the P&L, ask about your gross margins, EBITDA margins, where all the costs go, and what your top three cost components are. Be curious about why things are the way they are, with culture, operations, relationships, and finances.

Think about diagnosing, not changing. If you're talking about all the changes you're going to make, you're clearly not operating with a beginner's mind. In this initial stage, you're diagnosing the current state, focusing on what's working and what's not working. And be curious about why and how things might go differently if you made X or Y change. If you were a consultant brought in from the outside, what would you recommend and why? Where do you think the company should be in five years, and how do you think it should get there?

The caution here is you can't act on every single thing you hear, and you can't let anyone think you will. No one can drive more than five initiatives, and ideally the number is three or four.

With that said, when you're listening and you hear or observe, this early, that someone doesn't have the will/skill combination, you probably want to handle that immediately. If someone is low on wanting to do their job or being part of the team, in addition to low in skill level, that person needs to move out right away. The rest of the team is watching how you deal with low performance and culture fit. Everyone needs to be on board with the future strategy. Period.

3. *Present your findings.* After your ninety-day Listening Tour, you'll demonstrate you understand communications, culture, product, and people by presenting your findings. The company will feel like you've gotten to know them and what they care about.

You may have found a lack of clarity about purpose, vision, and values, and the next chapter will discuss how to work with that. When it's time for this meeting, you will have worked through any issues so you can present the company with the North Star you'll all be marching toward.

What to Look Out for during This Time

Anyone in this position can become overly consumed by their new role and fall out of whatever healthy norms and routines they had before. You have to do something for physical fitness and to maintain those workouts. And you can't neglect your mental fitness. Whether that's meditating, journaling, or both, being able to process what you're experiencing emotionally is crucial. How are you feeling? What emotions are dominant? What do you keep noticing about yourself? That element of self-reflection is critical. Of all of the situations I know of and have worked with, self-awareness makes or breaks them.

After reading so much about what successful people do to be more mindful and have more clarity, I kept running into journaling. In 2016, I gave it a try and never looked back. To this day, it's one of my best personal habits. I do daily gratitude journaling and a weekly reflective journal. The act of using pen to paper is one of the most underrated activities for clarity. And to be a great CEO, clarity has to be at the forefront for you and the direction you take your team.

Finally, socially, don't say yes to anything new. Don't join a new board or say yes to any new nonprofits. The only thing you want to say yes to is figuring out what's going on with the company you just took over. You're not going to have a bunch of extra time or bandwidth, so set yourself up for success and don't take on anything new.

Getting Down to Business

THE FIRST WEEKS

When I'm brought in to coach someone following a founder, I want to know how they define success. I ask three questions immediately, whether they have private shareholders, are owned by a private equity firm, or a mix:

1. Do you have a documented scorecard that tells you what the CEO of your new company needs to do?

2. Does that document have the key outcomes that drive shareholder value?

3. What's your cadence for reviewing your key outcomes with the board so you can all see if you're on track or off track?

New CEOs will frequently say they have those things but they don't have an actual scorecard. They may say, *I'm good—we don't need to do the scorecard thing because I know all about growing revenue, growing profit, and keeping clients happy.* But remember, it's more than that.

Back to Randy and Geoff, who literally wrote the book on score-cards: "They become the blueprint that links the theory of strategy to the reality of execution. Scorecards translate your business plans into role-by-role outcomes and create alignment among your team, and they unify your culture and ensure people understand your expecta-tions. No wonder they are such powerful management tools. Score-cards begin with your strategy."[2]

Remember that insisting on scorecards is a statement about what kind of leader you are. You're setting the tone for the whole company; you're creating a culture of accountability and transparency. It could be a bit of a shock to the team, depending on how loose the founder was. But your presence on the scene is the signal that the loosey-goosey days are over, and it's time to professionalize and scale. That's the priority.

If there's no scorecard, we either hire ghSMART if the CEO is open to that, or we make a scorecard together. We get input from the board and anyone else who can guide us in the creation of a final document that says these are the outcomes you're going to drive as the CEO, and here's how you're going to be held accountable. That "anyone else" includes other CEOs you know who will give you objective feedback on the role. World 50 has been invaluable for some of my clients.

This document you create isn't just for you. You cascade it into scorecards for the rest of the executive team, and then those cascade into every other role in the company. Everyone should have a scorecard. You need them for the positions you have now, as some of the people aren't a match for the positions they're in and you're going to have to find better fits.

Scorecards describe the mission for the position, outcomes that must be accomplished, and competencies that fit with both the culture of the company and the role. You wouldn't think of having someone

---

2   Geoff Smart and Randy Street, *Who* (Random House Publishing Group. Kindle Edition) 39–40.

build you a house without an architect's blueprint in hand. Don't think of hiring people for your team without this blueprint by your side.[3]

If you don't do a formal ghSMART-type assessment, it should probably take thirty days of back and forth with your board member or peer and some feedback from the CFO and a few other senior people to solidify your scorecard. And that helps everyone as it's a multiplier of sorts, as you can see. Once you have your scorecard, you can cascade that into scorecards for the rest of the executive team and then into the roles for everyone else in the company. Every role should have a scorecard.

If I could make a personal recommendation influencing what you end up doing, I would strongly suggest you get the scorecard done externally. Everybody's deficient in self-awareness. The most self-aware people I know still have blind spots; they're human. An outsider doesn't have to work against their own biases and subjectivity as much as an insider. It's far easier for them to get the job done without getting bogged down in history, personalities, and culture. As the saying goes, insiders know how the sausage is made, and that can be a liability that opens them up to focusing on the wrong thing and making assumptions, both positive and negative.

If you're an insider and it's not possible to get an outsider, you need to think like one. When you're from the outside, you're hyper-aware of everything. You're curious and you want to know what every-thing means and why it's done. Internal transitions often end up being sloppy because you tend to think you know too much, plus you're used to things being done a certain way. Just because they're done that way doesn't mean it's the best way or the most efficient way or the most effective way within the process or workflow as a whole. It's easy to look at or analyze things based on your biases, not realizing

---

3   Ibid.

you might not be looking at the right things, plus your biases are in the way when you do look.

Scorecard for CEO of Acme[JS7]
2024-2026

	KEY OUTCOMES

1.	*Deliver double-digit financial growth, achieving $200M in revenue by 2026.*
	
	• Grow revenue from ~$140M in 2024 to $200M in 2026, while maintaining margins in (at least) the 35–38 percent range.
	• Drive meaningful growth in both existing businesses, taking the:
	    > Core business from ~$xxM revenue in 2024 to $xxxM in 2026;
	    > Advisory business from ~$xxM ARR in 2024 to $xxxM in 2026.
	• Establish a new line of business (whether via organic or inorganic growth) and delivering ~$30M+ revenue by 2026.
	• Set milestones, establish operational plans, and partner with sponsors and the board to closely monitor financial results.

2.	*Maximize the value of Acme's portfolio by articulating and operationalizing a cross-sell strategy between the two business units.* • Work closely with presidents of consulting and advisory businesses to build out a cross-sell strategy, including both longer-term guiding principles and approach, as well as shorter-term tactical initiatives to drive conversion. • Hold consulting and advisory presidents accountable for operationalizing the strategy and remove roadblocks as needed ongoing. • By 20XX, drive an attach rate of advisory services after core consulting projects of XX percent and sell-in of core consulting projects to advisory clients of XX percent.

3.

Build an inorganic growth capability to consistently evaluate both incremental and transformative acquisition opportunities.

- Ensure the capabilities are in place to drive programmatic M&A, initially of tuck-in acquisitions, but also with an eye for more transformative opportunities (e.g., acquiring a similarly sized competitor).
- Define, build, and oversee the team required to manage a robust acquisition pipeline.
- Support thorough due diligence and the construction of sound business cases. Vet ideas with the board and leverage sponsors to structure and negotiate deals.
- Be a credible brand ambassador. Gain preference with sellers.
- Ensure seamless integration of acquisitions and on-time capture of expected revenue and cost synergies.

4.

Support acceleration of the advisory business while ensuring continued delivery of a strong client experience in the core consulting business.

- To accelerate the advisory business:
  - > Serve as a thought partner to BU president regarding highest-value commercial levers, encouraging commercial creativity and a Test & Learn mindset to try new things and make strategic pivots along the way.
  - > Ensure business has the Sales & Marketing engine and supporting team required to supercharge growth.
  - > Ensure robust decision-making process with regard to capital deployed to ensure return on investment of at least XX percent.
  - > Create a loyal and satisfied customer base with renewal rates of XX percent+.
- To deliver strong client experience in the core consulting business:
  - > Maintain average NPS scores >65. Track customer satisfaction and regularly discuss how to action the feedback.
  - > Ensure ~80 percent employee retention to support delivery.
  - > Foster a focus on delivering on commitments with quality.
  - > Continuously optimize the team and evolve delivery approaches in order to satisfy evolving customer needs.

5.	*Pursue ongoing business model innovations to create at least one successful new line of business by 2025.* • Oversee the innovation flywheel charged with regularly generating, exploring, and evaluating disruptive ideas to drive business growth. • Serve as a member of the investment committee charged to evaluate ~X-X ideas per quarter and be decisive in prioritizing high-potential ideas and deploying the necessary resources to support them.

6.	*Develop and strengthen a best-in-class executive leadership team.*
	
	• Initially and continuously evaluate the senior team to enhance talent and capabilities across all businesses, attaining >80 percent A-players in all key roles, by:
	   > Hiring and retaining A-players.
	   > Coaching and developing B-players.
	   > Swiftly redeploying or removing C-players.
	
	• Continuously improve talent development capabilities and supporting processes.
	
	• Support building a larger bench in core business to ensure a maximum utilization across cohorts of ~80 percent.
	
	• Evolve organizational structure as needed to support growing advisory business and new business model innovations.
	
	• Identify and develop X potential succession candidates by YY.
	
	• Implement an operating cadence that clarifies priorities, steers execution and decision-making rigor, and drives accountability to desired metrics.

Work collaboratively and transparently with the financial sponsors to deliver a successful outcome.

- Maximize company value by staying ahead of industry dynamics to deliver >3.5x ROI to investors.

- Take ownership for company performance. Set and communicate realistic targets and deliver on them reliably.

- Proactively communicate with and seek input from investors and board members on business opportunities and challenges.

7.
- Provide opinions and perspective with conviction, balanced with open-mindedness and a willingness to listen (i.e., relish advice and debate).

- Engender confidence and trust through proactivity, responsiveness, and transparency (no surprises).

- Convey a strong command of the business and key exit objectives in monthly calls and board meetings. Contribute to relevant exit activities, including participating in interactions with potential buyers.

- Influence board composition, as needed, and build trusting relationships with board members.

At the end of the first ninety days, you should be able to show your people your distilled results, in dashboard form, like this:

EMPLOYEES

START:

STOP:

CONTINUE:

MARKET

START:

STOP:

CONTINUE:

COMPANY PERFORMANCE

START:

STOP:

CONTINUE:

CUSTOMERS

START:

STOP:

CONTINUE:

KEY ACCELERANTS

→ Allow the first few moments and days to be about gratitude and processing any emotions and thoughts around this life transition.

→ Make sure every position has a scorecard.

→ Operate with a beginner's mind.

→ Position yourself for a Listening Tour. Let everyone know what you'll be doing and when you'll present your findings.

→ Don't change anything major, with the possible exception of your executive team, and that will be discussed in chapter 6.

Now that you have all this crucial information, you can start strategizing. Let's get into what that looks like, as well as who's going on this journey with you.

CULTURE CORNERSTONES: PURPOSE, VISION, VALUES

This chapter requires you to have an open mind. It involves words and concepts that people don't necessarily agree on. Culture means different things to different people. Meanwhile, some people use mission and values, and others use purpose and values. Some have visions rather than missions. I invite you to put your preconceived notions aside. If you don't, you might miss the fact that this chapter is really a road map to getting culture right. Right, in this case, means creating something scalable and repeatable.

When someone says to anyone at your company, "Tell me about your culture," every person should answer the same way. Culture is the result of everyone understanding and living the purpose, vision, and values. Here's how you make that happen.

Your ninety-day Listening Tour involves learning what your stakeholders think about who you are as a company, what you do, and why. Stakeholders include customers, employees, board members, and the competition. Your intention, again, is not to change anything (yet), but to get the lay of the land.

You likely know what the founder thinks because you've spent enough time with that person that you understand their perspective on culture. You've probably heard a sentence that begins with: *This is my dream—to go beyond what I built, to X.* Part of your job as Second CEO is to activate the founder's dream. You'll identify paths forward to what the founder thinks the business can become.

The only time the founder's perspective may not be as relevant is when they leave the business. Depending on the circumstances, the founder may be looking to detach themselves from the company. If I use my own example with Greg, he was committed to sharing what he believed SBI could become, as well as being an advocate beyond his departure. Every situation is different.

Knowledge of the founder's dream is only half the story, though. You need to establish what kind of alignment there is within the company, and within the ecosystem you operate. You do this by focusing part of your tour on understanding the cornerstones of culture—purpose, vision, and values. In this chapter, we'll discuss the refinement and shaping of culture, via company purpose, vision, and values. These are the bedrocks of shaping and evolving culture in any business, especially one where you are taking over from a founder-CEO.

Purpose

Purpose answers one question: *Why do you exist?* It's the original reason the company was founded. This is no longer a start-up. By now, you have empirical evidence for why you exist and how you've fared up to this point. That empirical evidence comes from: why clients hire you, why employees join you, and how you're different from competitors in terms of your unique value proposition. Your Listening Tour should reveal this valuable commentary.

Purpose is the Why behind what we do on a daily basis. It's the drumbeat.

Purpose should be communicated in a single sentence that everybody understands and rallies behind. And the purpose the founder had when they started the business might be different from what you believe the company can become now. Presumably, the company has grown and you're being brought in to professionalize and scale it. Purpose may have shifted a little or a lot, and that's OK. When crafting a purpose statement, focus on ensuring it's relevant, energizing, and the guiding light for why the company exists. This is where belief is fostered, and when things get rough, you want to be able to fall back on your purpose as a decision-making tool. It's the rudder of the boat. And many times, it's not well known across the company, or it's known, but not believed. Your Listening Tour will tell you where you stand.

Here are some sample purpose statements I find powerful:

- SBI—Drive people to reach their full potential.

- INSIGHT2PROFIT—Offer end-to-end solutions that achieve sustainable profit improvement.

- ghSMART—We help CEOs, boards, and investors move swiftly from strategy to results, practicing the art and science of building winning leadership teams.

- Collective 54—We help boutiques earn more, work less, and exit bigger (and faster).

Vision

Purpose is why you exist, and vision is *what* you can become. You understand, from the lens of the founder, what the initial vision was. And the founder may have also shared their vision of what the company can become under your leadership or "in a perfect world."

When you do your Listening Tour, you might find that people agree about what the vision is and operate with it as their North Star. In this case, nothing needs to change. Or maybe some execution needs to change, but the vision is otherwise intact. On the other hand, your feedback might be more like, *The vision was amazing and got the company to this point, but what got us here won't get us where we want to be.* In that case, the vision needs to change. Maybe it's more expansive now. Maybe the company has become more specialized or your offering set has expanded and needs a holistic fresh view of the value you create.

There are telltale signs of a vision that's wobbly and might be in need of revision, and the clearest one is an inconsistency between what the founder says and the way the employees are behaving. This tells you that either the vision hasn't stuck and changes need to be made, or the employees see possibilities the founder doesn't see, and maybe the employees are onto something.

Very often, there's a point during your Listening Tour where you recognize the purpose and vision aren't as codified by the employees as they need to be. This is OK and isn't an indictment or judgment of the founder. In fact, quite the opposite. Take this as an opportunity to rally the employee base around the art of the possible.

For example, for the longest time at SBI, our vision was to be "the McKinsey of sales." What did this mean? We rallied behind the fact that McKinsey is the preeminent brand in strategy consulting. We wanted to be the preeminent brand, but for sales/go-to-market-specific consulting. As I did my Listening Tour, I learned that the employees didn't feel moved by this anymore. Furthermore, SBI had moved beyond doing just sales; we were becoming a more holistic growth advisory firm that included marketing, pricing, and customer success.

Our vision became "the premier platform for accelerating revenue growth." We wanted to be the number one choice when a client/prospect was thinking, "How do I grow faster?" We wanted them to see our firm as a platform with a suite of services, and not just as a sales consulting firm. And to show you that visions can change, as I'm writing this book, SBI's vision is undergoing another change. Companies evolve as do visions.

Here are some vision statements I think are powerful and motivating.

- 3Pillar Global—A product development partner for scaling digital businesses. We provide solutions that align businesses with their customers and aspirations.

- ghSMART—Gives data and the perspective you need to influence positive change and create value faster.

- Alix Partners—Helping businesses respond to challenges when everything is on the line. Each project is different, but they all have one thing in common—a need for decisive, informed, and often urgent action.

- Bespoke Partners—To bring exceptional focus, expertise, and industry networks to recruiting, onboarding, and advising high-impact leaders in software and SaaS companies.

- Embark—Solving complex problems for finance functions. To build a world-class advisory firm that's just as much about people as it is about know-how and skill.

- Resolve Growth—To partner with entrepreneurs who wake up every day thinking about new challenges.

Values

Core values define how you behave. If the company has core values, and most do, pay attention to how often they're mentioned. Values should be something you can see in the day-to-day of how employees carry out their work. Here are some quick questions to help you answer, "Are our values alive?"

- How often do people talk about them?

- Are they part of the hiring process?

- Are they part of performance reviews?

- Are they part of terminations?

- Are they part of employee recognition?

- How do you see them on a daily basis and how do you talk about them?

- Do you talk about them on all-hands calls?

- Do you publish them for all the world to see but not really live them?

- Are the values alive?

Culture emerges from the unique combination of purpose, vision, and values. If the culture is alive, that tells you the values are being activated on a daily basis. And if that's what you see, that's fantastic, and no change is required.

Sometimes you'll notice that the values sound like the founder. This is understandable because founder-led businesses typically have a strong person at the helm, projecting their values. That frequently works well until it's time to scale. A non-founder-led business in a scaling stage will likely have different values. What values are necessary *now*? Moving into a different era doesn't mean you move on from all the traditions and rituals of the founder. You can still honor all of them, but through a different lens.

During your first ninety days, ask your people about the values of the firm. Ask if they're on display, and if so how? Where?

Values are nonnegotiable and anchoring. When everything goes sideways and you're wondering what to do, your values are your religion. And they need to be meaningful. Management consultant, author, and founder of the Table Group Patrick M. Lencioni writes, "Empty values statements create cynical and dispirited employees, alienate customers, and undermine managerial credibility."[4]

WHAT MAKES A GOOD VALUE?

What makes a good value is you can use it in a sentence and you can catch somebody behaving that way. For example, let's say one of your values was "build the firm—embrace teamwork to build something greater than ourselves." Something you might hear at a meeting is, *Hey, James. I love the way you build the firm by helping new employees. You're always embracing teamwork to ensure others are getting the most out of their time here, and I really appreciate that.*

---

4   Patrick M. Lencioni, "Make Your Values Mean Something," *Harvard Business Review*, July 2002, https://hbr.org/2002/07/make-your-values-mean-something.

Look at it this way: the way your best employees behave—you want everybody to behave like that. And you want to always be uplifting and formally recognizing those who display the firm's values, including details about how they're doing it.

The values need to be part of the fabric of the organization. Not just, *Yeah, we have values, but nobody knows what they are.* You want to spotlight a value each day and talk about someone who embodies it. That should be a norm for how you operate.

If you're asking, *How do we operationalize living our values each day?* the answer is daily huddles/stand-ups. I'm a big fan of the book and material in *Scaling Up,* by Verne Harnish. I love the simplicity of how Verne lays out a good value-reinforcement cadence. Each day, your employees should be in a ten- to fifteen-minute huddle or stand-up. This call is probably first thing in the morning. On this call:

1. Somebody nominates a person in the company for living a value. They read the definition of the value, and share why the nominee embodies it. Simple, but powerful. And a daily habit.

2. Each employee shares good news from the previous twenty-four hours.

3. Each employee shares the most important thing they need to do for the next twenty-four hours.

4. Each employee shares an area where they're stuck/hitting a roadblock. *Why?* The coach/manager of the group needs to hear where people are struggling. You don't problem-solve in the huddle. However, as the leader, you're listening for the *stucks,* and when you hear the same thing from a few people or over a few days, you know there's a bottleneck in the company. And from there, you can do real problem-solving

with leadership. This improves leadership and execution velocity.

Here are some values I think are particularly powerful:

SBI:

- Be great—Strive for excellence, and continually aspire to a higher standard.

- Adopt a growth mindset—Acquire new capabilities, embrace new ideas, and seek out diverse experiences.

- Own the outcome—Hold yourself accountable to find the solution for both teammates and clients.

- Build the firm—Embrace teamwork to build something greater than ourselves.

- Inspire others—Empower those around you and transfer positive energy to clients and peers.

- Embrace 1:1—Invest in relationships that will endure for decades.

Bespoke Partners:

- Invest in others' success—Foster a team-first environment. Actively support others in reaching their potential. Recognize that client success is our success.

- Be memorable—Be your authentic self. Take every opportunity to leave a positive, lasting impression on others. Go above and beyond to deliver an exceptional and differentiated experience to our clients and candidates.

- Inspire growth—Never accept the status quo. Lean into a growth mindset and demonstrate learning agility. Seek out new approaches to solve problems.

- Winners win—Be resilient and optimistic. Always look for the silver lining and find opportunity in challenging situations. Extract lessons from both successes and failures.

Resolve Growth:

- Honesty—Authenticity and transparency at all times. Willingness to constructively challenge each other. Build trust and respect through our time in the trenches together.

- Hunger—Relentless drive to make your business even more successful. Speed of responsiveness and decision-making. Grit and resilience.

- Humility—Egos checked at the front door. Self-awareness and ability to acknowledge our limitations. Growth mindset and orientation toward continuous improvement.

WHEN YOU NEED TO UPDATE VALUES

There are various reasons you might need to revise your values or maybe swap one out. Principal among them is a new leader shepherding in a new stage of growth for the company. In other words, it could be entirely appropriate for *you* to change one or all of the values. Remember that the values of a founder-led business usually coincide with the personality of the founder. But when you're scaling the company and entering a new chapter of leadership, you want to work as a team to identify values that will take you where you want to go next.

The way to change them is to form a small group I call a Culture Committee, composed of your top performers. Ask them, *What is it about our top employees that we love? Why do we want more Nicks and Kristens? What do these people do that's so inspiring, helpful, or effective?* Maybe it's their competitive urgency or how diligently they follow up on details. The feedback from the Culture Committee will give you your new values.

Culture

Culture is an emergent property. If your purpose, vision, and values are lived by your people, what arises as a result of their synergy is the company culture. It's not a separate thing; it comes from the three cornerstones everyone knows about and agrees to embody in the way they relate, communicate, and work.

An example we used during my time leading SBI was: I would observe new hires asking employees to "describe the culture" or articulate "what's the culture like?" I believe this is a critical question for new hires and for existing employees to ask. However, most companies don't have a consistent way to answer. As a result, you get myriad answers to something that should be consistent and certain. Meanwhile, most companies I see don't have consistency. That lack of consistency makes it difficult for people to truly live the culture; they can't define it. At SBI, when somebody said, "Tell me about your culture," our response was, "We are purpose-driven, vision-focused, and values-based." And from there, all employees could recite the purpose, vision, and core values. Each employee carried a values card with them at all times, which was a tradition started by Greg and continued during my leadership tenure.

Without this level of focus and follow-through, you'll have cultural inconsistency. You can see how the response to *Tell me about your culture* can become super squishy, super quickly, if you don't have your purpose, vision, and values down. As a CEO, *YOU are the culture champion*. Not the head of HR. You.

If the question following *Tell me about your culture* is *What does that look like on a daily basis?* what are you going to say? Here's what you want to be able to say:

You see the purpose on display in how people are thinking about serving clients and serving each other. You see the vision on display because whenever people get discouraged, they remind themselves of the world they're working to create. And you see the values on display, daily, in how people communicate with each other and do their jobs.

All of that is going smoothly—your culture is defined and alive—when before a hiring decision is made, people are rating a new potential employee against the values. Or the values are used in performance reviews. Or employees who aren't consistent with the values are terminated. Or your annual recognition is based on a vote for people who display your core values. That's how you know your values are aligned and alive.

Lastly, you should be talking about your values on a daily basis, and peers should be reinforcing the displays of values they witness. You want the values to cascade throughout the company, and if there's pushback about how everyone should be behaving, lean into that pushback and be curious about it. Take the most outspoken-but-trustworthy naysayer and bring them into the Culture Committee. Allow their voice to be heard, and see if there's something to what they're saying. Be open and receptive to their experience.

A WORD OF CAUTION FOR THOSE HIRED FROM WITHIN

When you're hired from within, there's a temptation to say, *I know all this. I was part of shaping the culture, and we're good. I don't need a Listening Tour.* Resist that urge, and instead, be judicious because you're no longer the Number Two or in whatever other role. You're now the CEO. You're the leader, and you need to be thoughtful and thorough. And even if you don't make any changes, which is highly doubtful, the employees will appreciate your diligence and the fact that you're acting with a beginner's mind. That's how you create loyalty and connectivity to you.

Common Mistakes

1. Doing all this in a vacuum and only considering executive feedback.

2. Doing all this in a vacuum and only considering the feedback of a small group of veterans rather than getting a diverse cross-section of roles and people. You want this to reflect what the company can become, not what it was. So honor the old, but be focused on the art of the possible. As you'll see in the next chapter, your focus is on where you can go and thinking future back from there, not on moving forward in the same way you've been moving.

3. Not reading client feedback, employee exit interviews, and employee engagement studies to help you understand how clients and employees feel about the firm.

Of all the parts of your Listening Tour, going up and down the organization for employee feedback of star employees, by role and prioritizing diversity, is probably the most important. Those are the people who will become your cultural champions and will appreciate you digging in and asking questions. Engaging them cascades and builds momentum for your vision.

How do you identify these people if you're from the outside? If you have a scorecard, you're looking for people who not only deliver results, but do it the right way. So you're looking not only at outcomes, but at behaviors. Who gets both right?

The Clients' Perspective

Client feedback is critical to this process, as the internal narrative regarding how clients view you doesn't always map onto their actual thoughts, feelings, and experiences. What questions should you be asking your clients?

1. Why are your best clients your best clients? And how do you get more of them? What's the unique value proposition you bring that you can do more of?

2. Why are you the brand of choice or Number Two? What's your right to win in the market? When compared with your competitors, what is it about what you do that they either can't do or are unwilling to do? That's where you have competitive differentiation.

3. What could you be doing that would separate you from your competitors even more? What are you not doing that you need to be doing?

Caveat: If you're dealing with a younger company, it's possible that there aren't systems for customer, employee, or competition feedback and research. If that's the case, that will be something you'll need to bake into your strategic plan (the next chapter).

KEY ACCELERANTS

→ Purpose is the WHY behind what you do on a daily basis.

→ Vision is what you can become; it's your North Star.

→ Values are how you behave.

→ Culture arises from the synergy of purpose, vision, and values.

→ Form a Culture Committee that's diverse and includes naysayers.

→ Include the perspective of your clients.

→ Behave like you're from the outside. That mindset will help you be receptive and thorough.

STRATEGY: WHERE TO PLAY AND HOW TO WIN

The core challenge for the CEO is balancing taking care of the near term while planning for the future. I think about this through a Two-Horizon framework.[5] Horizon One is the first twelve months in the job. Horizon Two is your three- to five-year value creation plan (VCP). This includes you clearly articulating what you want the business to look like and who is sitting around the table as part of your executive team.

Horizon One

In the research for this book, I asked founders, successors, and private equity investors how much time the most successful CEOs spend on

5   Mehrdad Baghai, Steve Coley, and David White, *The Alchemy of Growth: Practical Insights for Building the Enduring Enterprise* (Basic Books, 2000).

McKinsey's Three-Horizon Model Is Described in this book. Horizon One was generally the first year, Horizon Two was years two and three, and Horizon Three was thirty-six to seventy-two months out. The model is thought by many to be outdated, as the pace of change is no longer measured in years and can happen at any time.

Horizon One thinking and operating in the first year. The consensus was around 70–80 percent. One of the partners who has spent almost three decades in private equity states, "You need to go all the way to the bottom of the pool, touch it, and then come back up as an effective CEO following the founder."

Going all the way to the bottom of the pool is your Listening Tour. Your thinking and decision-making around process, structure, and people, in order to set the company on its course (i.e., Horizon Two), come from listening in that first ninety days. You get a sense of the current state by talking to customers and employees, and understanding the market. In your second quarter, you decide whether the current strategy is the right one to bring the company's vision to life, or if it needs revising (more on that in a bit).

Because of the capacity and drive of the founder, you're usually walking into a situation where there are more things on the company's plate than it can handle. You have some decisions to make. And that's natural as Horizon One always involves some reacting. You can't anticipate many things that happen because you're new and you can't know everything. During your Listening Tour, you may have discovered the company is trying to do too many things, no one is sure what the competitive differentiator is, or the founder had pet projects that don't fit the purpose of the company and those projects need to go.

You heard a lot of good ideas on your tour, too. But part of the CEO's job is to say no to the good ideas so you can say yes to the great ones. Your number one job is to allocate human capital and financial capital to drive value creation. That's the essence of ensuring you have strategy done correctly.

Your people (including the board, and more about them in chapter 10), combined with the competitive analysis, will likely tell you where and how you should be playing so you'll win. My only caveat here is that sometimes the feedback you get is wildly different from what the founder told you. That could be a slippery slope. This is where data and facts, not hearsay and instinct, become critical. When in doubt, lean on the data. And if you don't have any, get some. It might take you a bit longer, and it might involve an objective third party, but you want to get to the end of the first six months and be able to deliver a strategy. Maybe it's just like the original one and maybe it's reimagined. Either way, you need to have a solid case for it and to communicate it clearly and effectively.

Simon Freakley, the CEO of management consulting firm Alix Partners, is on his third tenure as a CEO. He has built businesses, sold them, and even been asked to be the CEO of the firm he sold his business to. Here's what he had to say about the significance of the Listening Tour to the second quarter and strategy:

"What people want to know is that you've sought to understand the situation before you make changes. If they think you're making changes based on an inadequate understanding of the facts or the realities, you start to lose traction because they think you're not committed to understanding before you act. The Listening Tour is showing that you've heard people because you repeat back to them what you actually heard them say. What then happens, in my experience, if you go on to make changes, at least they know you've made them with full knowledge of what *they* believe to be the facts.

"I always say that a chief executive has to be their own Chief Communication Officer. You have to work out what the key messages are that need to be communicated that will give people a sense of who you are and what's important to you. Communicating where the company is and where you see it being able to get to is a worthy and purposeful objective. But it's not enough. They need to hear why they should feel the objective is a worthy and purposeful use of their time.

You need to be able to express that to the employees, to the clients, and to the other stakeholders.

"You're assembling all the information in the first ninety days, while in the back of your mind thinking, *What are the strategic priorities of the business to enable it to continue on its journey of growth and development?* While growth is often characterized as being a revenue number, the revenue is the lagging indicator of success. The leading indicator of success is *Do you have the right people doing the right work?* So you're looking for what the strategic priorities are for the firm to fulfill its ambition—or at least fulfill the next leg of the journey—and whether you feel that the elements are in place to make that possible.

"But of course, before you start laying that out, you do have to work out where the opportunities are. What's the point on the horizon you want people to galvanize around and drive toward? What are the rewards for getting there? And what are some of the twists and turns on the way and how do you get people thinking about those things? During that listening journey, you end up identifying things that need to be doubled down on, things that need to be fixed, and things that should change."

Do you see what Simon did there? It bears repeating.

> "You're assembling all the information in the first ninety days, while in the back of your mind thinking, *What are the strategic priorities of the business to enable it to continue on its journey of growth and development?*"

That's holding both horizons in your mind. In Horizon One, the day-to-day is coming at you and you can't hide from it. That requires a lot of attention. For you to be able to properly lay out what Horizon Two will be, you need a thorough understanding of how the business operates, and also put some points on the board in the first year. The power of quick wins cannot be understated. Think about these as "no-regret decisions" that will move the company along. The most complex part of being a CEO is how you straddle Horizons One and Two. And this never goes away; you just become more adept at navigating it.

Another built-in challenge when following a founder is a lot of decisions, and day-to-day operating and cultural norms, originated from that person. This isn't an indictment; it's just information. But it puts you in a delicate position. You can't shock the company too much by trying to be an "all strategy, all the time" CEO too early. Instead, you need to walk beside the founder. You must embrace and respect their scrappy nature—and that respect needs to be obvious to everyone—*while* determining your methodical plan to evolve.

As that first year comes to an end, you'll start to see your time allocation shift, where you're spending more like 40–50 percent of your time in Horizon One. At this point, we're talking about near-term things your functional leaders should be running. You're the conductor; you don't play an instrument. You might be asking, *Why do I need to spend half of my time in the day-to-day?* Because that's where your team is living. And for you to be an effective coach, you need enough feel and proximity to running the day-to-day. As my coach, Tim Stratman, says, "When you're a leader, you're achieving through other people. It's not about you under the hood, fixing things. It's about you running the pit crew. And it's about developing people."

Meanwhile, you also need to carve out purposeful time in your calendar to work *on* the business rather than *in* the business. You need that solid VCP for the next three to five years. And you have to be able to clearly communicate the course you've charted to the next milestone.

When I asked Second CEOs how to ensure they did this, the overwhelming response was *discipline*. This includes sacred time on your calendar, blocked out, that no one can touch. Not one call or meeting. Tim Stratman told me, "The best CEOs I work with have two blocks of four to five hours per week that are titled 'think time.'" Whether this is Tuesday and Friday morning from 8 to 12, or afternoons, CEOs need margin. Your time is never your own when you're in the role, but you do have the power to carve out time. You can't take your eye off of Horizon Two and a suggestion from my coach is using your "think time" to status-check progress on Horizon Two objectives once per month. Make this a habit. There will be a natural cadence of quarterly offsites, board meetings, lender updates, and PE firm strategy sessions. These will ensure your focus on the Horizon Two plan.

All those meetings should help train your mindset about Horizon Two, which is crucial to your success. If you're owned by a private equity firm, taking your eye off of Horizon Two equals failure. Investors expect you to answer how you'll make good on their investment. Make no mistake about it—PE firms hire you to deliver an outcome. It's your job as the CEO to return capital to shareholders. Full stop.

Here's Dave Tayeh, Head of North American Private Equity for Investcorp:

"We're generally five-year investors, which, compared to the public markets, is a long time. But it's amazing how fast twenty quarters go. We also say: *We've got twenty quarters, and we want to compound our money at 25 percent a year. So day one, if you're not compounding 25 percent, you're actually going backward.* The CEO needs to understand how their investors are thinking, and this may sound obvious, but you'd be shocked how often that's not the case. There needs to be clarity in communication and alignment on what we're trying to achieve." (You'll hear from Dave again in chapter 10 when I discuss your relationship with the board.)

The key lenses: the competitive feedback, employee feedback, client feedback, and then the overall market that you plan and that's the four-lens Venn diagram that people should take into consideration.

Horizon Two: Your Strategy

Strategy is a question that needs to be answered by the CEO. And the information required to properly and thoroughly answer it comes from listening. So the outcome of the Listening Tour is strategy. After your tour, you have one question . . .

Do we have the right strategy in place to activate and fulfill our vision?

Outcome #1—*Yes.* Then move to the execution of that strategy.

Outcome #2—*No, not really, almost-but-not-quite,* and any other version that isn't a complete *Yes.*

This is by far the most common situation, where the strategy needs some refinement. It's your job to refine it.

Strategy, simply put, is where to play and how to win.

How to Bring Your Vision to Life, Step by Step

Although I spent much of my first year as CEO making quick moves and not communicating well, I did eventually get my bearings. The team around me ensured we had the right strategy, improved systems, and refined processes that set the foundation for continued growth in revenue and EBITDA as a rule-of-55 firm (i.e., a combination of growth rate and profit percentage that equals 55. For example, 20 percent growth and 35 percent EBITDA is the rule of 55).

Here's how I did it: The Strategy One-Pager.

Visions, by nature, articulate what success looks like in the future. They're succinct and there's no How mentioned. To translate vision into a strategy that's codified, easily communicated, and actionable, you need to work *future back,* creating the conditions and processes that combine to activate the vision. You're answering the question, *What would I have to do next to work my way to that three- to five-year goal?*

The answers to those questions should be able to fit on one page. The one-pager is the culmination of a four-part process that lays out the year for all to see.

1. Visions tend to be abstract. Aspirations, on the other hand, are concrete. They're not the only ways to reach the vision, but they're the ways that strike you as doable based on what you're already succeeding at, and the feedback from your stakeholders.

   An example of one set of aspirations from a CEO we spoke to were:

   - 83 percent employee retention

   - $50M in recurring revenue

   - $250M total revenue

   - 33 percent EBITDA

   - 3.5x ROIC (return on invested capital)

This kind of structure of metrics will be appropriate for most companies. They're not really SMART (Specific, Measurable, Attainable, Relevant, Time-bound) goals, as they should be outside your comfort zone, which means attainable isn't assumed. That's why they're aspirational; you shouldn't easily be on track to easily achieve them. You're going to have to work hard, innovate, and be the best.

2. What are the strategic initiatives that set you up to achieve your aspirational goals?

3. Explore the strategic initiatives one at a time. What capabilities and enablers are necessary inputs? How do you create an environment where, for instance, you can deliver the kind of client experience you strive for and be positioned to grow the business? In this case, our job is to acquire, engage, and retain top talent. But that won't do the job without a good digital product and solution platform. And all of that isn't complete without the research and content production engine.

Capabilities and enablers are typically the functional elements, such as HR, research/innovation, or the technology product function. They're disciplines that report to the CEO and are critical for enabling the customer-facing elements to come to life.

Whether you're a product company or a service company, you need to address how you're going to generate more new business and continue to drive new market share. Depending on your purpose, you might also be thinking about how you're going to shift your client experience so you have clients and customers for life.

4. None of the above tells you the rhythm or the cadence of what's happening daily, monthly, or quarterly. For that, you need an operating model, which tells you the management method you'll be using.

I'm sure you've seen all the books and the courses. You may recall I recommended *Scaling Up* by Verne Harnish in chapter 5. I've also mentioned EOS (Entrepreneurial Operating System), and I'm a big fan of it. Choosing an operating model or management model is important, but more important, from a strategic standpoint, is spreading it through the company. Whichever system you choose is the governance by which you run the business. And you can get much more scale if you're committed to sticking with your choice. I think of it this way: if you want to get into better shape and you decide you're going to do CrossFit instead of being a triathlete, do that. Stick to it. You don't have to do both. Just pick something that works for you, and be consistent with the execution of whatever fitness model you're using. It's the exact same thing for running your company.

We hired a company called Innosight to help us create our one-pagers, and here's what they came up with.

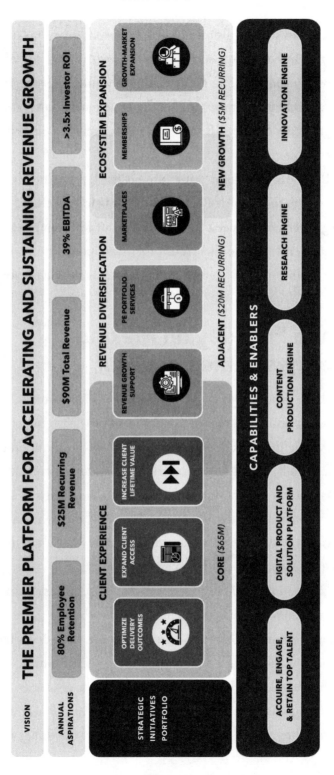

You can see our vision up top. The aspirations we have that sit underneath that vision and they're quantified, and there's one for employee retention, one for recurring revenue, and one for profitability. Underneath that are the key strategic initiatives that we're going to drive. So for SBI, there was client experience and three ways we were going to drive it.

The most important things are on the left side of the conveyor belt going to the right side of the conveyor belt. And this is part of the strategic debate you need to have with your leadership team—what truly matters from the client/customer standpoint.

If all this sounds like you're about to make changes, you are.

Simon Freakley on Making Changes in the First Year

"You have your biggest and best opportunity to make necessary changes in your first year as CEO. You don't leave big changes till Year Two or Year Three because you've lost the honeymoon period in which to do it. So you have to work it out reasonably quickly but not too fast; not in the first hundred days. If there's a crisis or something urgent or something that's so blatantly wrong, then you have to do it because if you don't do it, it then compromises you. But in the absence of that, take the first quarter to get your bearings.

"The founder might be around, maybe acting as chairman, and they might have quite a lot of emotional attachment to the decisions that had been made before you arrived. Quietly but deliberately, you have to be working with the founder in the background to make sure that they're going to be either vocal in support or at least not speak out against what you're trying to do. Otherwise, of course, you end up being interrupted and not being able to get the things done.

"And the board will expect you to communicate your strategy after one hundred days. And then to a leadership team, and then it would work out through town halls. This is all part of being the chief communications officer—telling everyone there's going to be a new strategy. They want to know, once you've got your bearings, what your plan is. When people ask you, *What's your strategy?* what they're really asking is, *Where are we going? And what are your expectations of me? Because then I know what it takes to be successful.*"

Common Mistakes

- You're leaping into action, like I did when I succeeded Greg, without an actual strategy and without communicating what you'll be doing and why.

- You're not taking enough time to whittle down the most important elements of the company strategy into a format people can understand. Typically, this looks like a strategy that's too broad.

- Your strategy has a lot of "intuition" and "gut-based" language rather than being fact-based.

- Your strategy isn't codified in a way that the rest of the organization can understand. Strategies activate visions. If the vision isn't being brought to life with the way you communicate and codify the strategy, confusion will result. Confusion means no buy-in, and no buy-in means no dedication to collectively moving forward toward a common goal.

- You're thinking present forward. Rather than asking, in a vacuum, what you should be doing next, pick a milestone that's three to five years in front of you. Your strategy is best designed by asking, *What would be the next thing I would be doing if I were to reach that milestone?* That kind of thinking is called *future-back* thinking, and it's what professional futurists do. It's more expansive and surfaces possibilities more than thinking present forward.

- You're *planning too ambitiously*, and it is disconnected from where the business is today. Sometimes a CEO comes in and paints this picture, a quarter in, of where they're going to take the business in three years, and it's totally divorced from reality. There's no viable path to get from here to there. People can't see how to get there and the CEO loses credibility.

KEY ACCELERANTS

Here are the milestones you have to hit to maintain momentum through the end of your first year as Second CEO to accelerate scale:

→ You've learned about and stabilized the key components of running your particular business as a CEO.

→ You've ensured purpose, vision, and values are defined.

→ You've reconstituted the three- to five-year strategy to ensure where you play and how you win is the foundation of your strategy.

→ You have an understanding of your core processes, including which ones are working and which ones aren't (more on that in chapter 7).

→ You have an optimized organizational structure that allows you to set the company up in the friendliest and friction-free way for customers and employees (details in chapter 8).

→ You've built a team and created a people function that's full of A-players who can take you to the next North Star on your road map (I'll show you how in chapter 9).

Once you understand strategy, think about what processes you need to run alongside each of your strategies or capabilities. Next, we'll map out the processes you have and don't have. Don't skip this next step because you're afraid of what you might find.

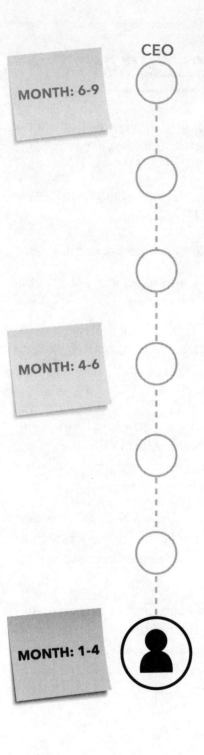

THE CONTINUOUS NATURE OF PROCESSES

Once the Second CEO knows what they want to achieve strategically, it's time to build processes to support that work. The thing about processes, if you're in a growth and scaling mode, is that they're probably the least static part of the business. Between *what got you here won't get you there* and technical innovations (which affect some industries more than others), you need to be nimble. Your goals are to get everything working as best it can and have the people and the mindsets in place to bob and weave when you need to. I think of processes as having three phases: initial discovery, documentation, and then iteration based on new information. The first two phases get done in the second half of Year One, and the rest of your tenure is all about iteration.

Phase One: Discovery

Processes are the key to creating scale. If you want to grow quickly and relatively effortlessly, there is one thing you can't do without—standardized processes that allow average people to perform at an above-average level. If you're reading this and wondering, *Who wakes up wanting to be average?* the answer is very few people. However, all companies have a classic mix of performers:

- the top 15–20 percent, who are great at what they do and require little supervision;

- the bottom 10–15 percent, who aren't the right fit and don't execute as you wish; and

- the middle 60–70 percent.

The key to creating outsized value as a leader is moving the middle. You must create an environment where an average performer can perform at an above-average rate. What's the cornerstone of such an environment? Replicable, detailed, codified processes.

Is this a nonnegotiable? Everything seems to be going well!

Things might be going well now, but the moment there are bottlenecks and something isn't going well, you're left with anecdotes. Anecdotes are a red flag. They show up when you can't look at a process and move through it, step by step, to figure out what went wrong. Everyone has a narrative about why things went sideways. And after all the stories, you still don't know what the process should be, so you still don't really know what went wrong.

For example, most companies have a selling process for acquiring new clients. Let's say you're doing your Listening Tour, you're looking at metrics, and you observe that the company is struggling to win new clients. You want to know why. Your first question is, "Do we have a sales process we're following for new client acquisition, and is it different from the process we use for selling more to existing customers?" Let's assume the answer is yes, you have a process. Don't take anyone's word for it. Look at the process, from the perspective of an outsider, and see if you can determine where things are breaking down.

If the answer is no, although it might be tempting to listen to the stories, that's not a good use of your time. What you want is a process. *How do you get it?* The same way you get all the others.

Phase Two: Documentation

To learn how each function is run, ask each of your functional leaders what three to five processes drive repeatability and scalability. This forces them to be methodical, structured thinkers. They have to identify their KPIs and the processes that drive those metrics.

For the client acquisition process, perhaps you're not targeting the right new clients, so that's what you need to work on. Perhaps it's the middle of the process, when you're introducing prospects to your capabilities or your product. Maybe the demonstration of that isn't going well. Then again, maybe the problem is happening at the end of the process, when you're talking about terms and your pricing isn't competitive. But until you get all of those steps down in their ideal fashion, you're not going to know what's broken.

Rather than just saying, "We're not winning new clients and we have to get better," pinpoint the breakdown. And if the new client acquisition process seems like it went according to plan, you have other information at your disposal to detect the problem. You can look for patterns across your functions. Maybe there are teamwork issues. Maybe you don't have a good management cadence. Maybe HR doesn't know what finance is working on because you don't publish goals. Get to the root cause.

And get specific about that root cause. I recently spoke with John Myers, the CEO of a large business called Rentokil, which just bought Terminix. John followed a founder when he walked into Rentokil, which had unique challenges of its own and a strong culture to work with. One of the things he does is asks each leader, "What problems are you trying to fix right now? And what's the data you're using to tell yourself that's a problem?" I thought that was really helpful. He also said something brilliant but simple and obvious—leaders have a tendency to have process on areas where they have comfort. So make sure you look holistically with your direct reports (CFO, CMO, CTO, etc.) to determine how a function is working, and where you have process gaps. Be thorough and ask all the annoying, probing questions that make people uncomfortable because they don't have the answers. And don't forget the data.

Whether your functional leaders need to revise processes or start from scratch because they've never had any, this must be done. You can't know where the gaps are until you've mapped all the process information you can possibly get in those critical first two quarters. Processes are your backbone. Plus, this is a valuable window into how your leaders work. You get to observe their level of organization, clarity, communication, and expertise. This observation will come in handy in chapter 8 when we discuss organizational structure.

Wait, back up, so all of this is supposed to be in writing?

Yes.

With that said, it's usually not, and this is the perfect opportunity to change that. Part of having a management method as a CEO is knowing how the company runs. And no one should be expected to keep all of that in their head—at least not at first.

Don't be surprised if you're starting from scratch.

Because you're following a founder, don't be surprised if there aren't a lot of processes in place. Founders tend not to be structured, process-driven people. They're dreamers and visionaries; all that process stuff is boring to them. The reason they started the company and were able to lead it through the series of firsts is because they love hard, right turns. They work very quickly and they have incredible instincts that can't be taught and scaled. And that's what you need when you're small. The heroic efforts of a few early hires who are committed to the vision and committed to the founder personally have much to do with early success. This, however, doesn't create scale.

Now in some cases, if the founder hired a COO or chief of staff, you may see more process than you expect. But in my experience, you're probably going to be overseeing the design/documentation of processes. And that's a fine position to be in, as sometimes it's easier to create something from scratch than fix something that's broken. Also, this gives you a wonderful opportunity to work directly with your new team, both one-on-one and in groups, and be a thoughtful teacher and collaborator. This is a time where being effective (i.e., taking your time) is more important than being efficient (i.e., rushing something out the door).

The job of the Second CEO is to think about scale and acceleration. Always be thinking, *How do I continue to drive repeatability and not a series of individual superstars?* Founders think they're superstars, but it's time for the majority of the company to shine instead, through their competence and consistency.

Regardless of what your leaders say about having to document their three to five processes or how they say it, be empathetic. You might even be able to put some quick wins in place by greenlighting something that the founder wouldn't—something employees have been waiting on but the founder was opposed to. You do this because you believe in it and you eventually would have done it, but the timing is different because it makes working at the company during this big transition a little easier. Plus, leaders who feel like their requests are falling on deaf ears feel demoralized. Quick wins boost morale. And boosting morale is helpful in the presence of resistance.

Phase Three: Iteration

Alex Shootman, the CEO of Alkami Technology, has followed four founders. He's fond of saying, when it comes to processes, "Everything is broken all the time." What he means is that if you try to build the perfect process for today, it will be outdated tomorrow. What you have to do instead is build and test. Then from there, you learn and adjust to all the variables that are constantly changing. This is truer for software companies than professional services companies, but there's so much wisdom in it. We should all be prepared to shift and adjust when pertinent new information comes our way. This is the concept of testing your assumptions constantly and rapidly. Let the organization see you promote a culture of rapid iteration.

We're coming up on the middle of your first year, and the organization is looking for you to maintain momentum and to demonstrate how you'll lead through change. That doesn't mean you make change for the sake of it, but there's going to be a natural anticipation. And when material information surfaces, all eyes are on you for how you're going to handle it. So get your facts, be methodical, and formulate whatever processes you need, while emphasizing the need for flexibility. Emerge with:

- a list of functional accountabilities;

- the most important metrics in each function that drive value; and

- which process each metric is attached to.

That's what you're looking for. That's the Holy Grail. Then tell everyone what you're going to do, why, and over what time period.

Remember what Simon Freakley said about change: You can't rush it, but you also can't wait until Year Two. The skillful way to do it is to listen while also observing how the company operates. You're looking for alignment across functions, detailed processes, data, and where your C-suite is getting stuck. You want to surface the gaps. You're looking to understand what your customers and employees think about your people, processes, and product. Finally, you're looking for the one part of your process that tends to change the most or be most affected by outside factors. This information is the foundation for the remediation plan you're going to introduce in the back half of Year One that you'll run into Year Two.

FUNCTION	FUNCTION OWNER	PROCESSES	HEALTH / MATURITY
Head of Company	CEO	Corporate Strategy	
		BOD Communication	
		Company Communication	
		ELT Development	
		ELT Operating Rhythm	
Strategy		M&A	
		Global Presence	
		Partnerships	
		Solution Packaging & Pricing	
Sales & Marketing		New Logo Acqusition Process	
		Vertical Marketing	
		Revenue Marketing	
		Expansion Revenue	
		Enablement	
Customer Success		Cross Sell	
		Net Promoter Score	
		Upsell	
		Customer Onboarding	
		Customer Retention	
		Staffing	
Product		Engineering	
		UI/UX	
		Product Thought Leadership	
		Product Marketing	
		Product Onboarding	
		Product Engagement	
		User Feedback	
Operations		PMO / Operating Governance	
		Technology / Data Management	
		Vendor Management	
		Analytics / Report Generation (Ops)	
		Hardware Management (Laptops)	
		Employee Administration	
		Legal Oversight / Reviews	
Finance		Financial Reporting	
		Budgeting	
		Back Office Infrastructure	
		Active Financial Management	
		Accounting / Administration / Monthly Closing	
		Accounts Payable	
		Accounts Receivable	

PROCESS OWNER	KPIS

FUNCTION	FUNCTION OWNER	PROCESSES	HEALTH / MATURITY
Finance		Payroll	
		Expense Processing	
		Audit	
		Taxes	
		Investor / Lender Relationship Management	
		Cash Management	
People		Recruiting	
		New Hires / Onboarding	
		Leadership Development	
		Performance Management	
		Compensation & Benefits	
		HR Operations (Exits, Systems, Compliance, ER)	
		Culture	
Corporate Marketing		Customer Advisory Councils	
		Communications	
		Brand Campaigns	
		Performance Analysis/Optimization	

FUNCTION:

High level areas of the business.

PROCESSES:

What we do within functions.

INITIATIVE:

Incremental improvements to processes within a function.

PROCESS OWNER	KPIS

Common Road Hazards

- Most newly minted CEOs move a little too fast. They make quick changes instead of being mindful and getting the full picture, just like I did at SBI. As a result, I whipsawed the company and had to go back and sort of slow things down. So make sure you balance having a true holistic understanding and putting trust in your leadership team. This is a time when you're going slow to go fast, correctly.

- You might get resistance from the leadership team.

  - If you've come from the outside, you'll hear things like:

    → "That's not really what our culture is all about."

    → "Our competitors don't do that. Why are you having to spend time on something like this?"

  - Meanwhile, if you come from the inside, it'll be:

    → "Hey, why are you changing? You didn't do that and ask for that when you were working with us as a peer! Why are you making us do that now?"

    → "Why are you micromanaging us?"

  - If you come from the outside:

    → Don't reference the way things worked at your old company.

    → Get a thorough understanding of the cultural norms and the way the company got successful. Don't make the mistake of throwing everything out and saying, "That's not how we're doing it under my watch!" Respect the past while understanding your role in building the future.

→ I've said it before, but ask five questions to every one statement that you give. Be a curious tourist in a familiar museum.

Prioritizing the understanding and documenting of your processes needs to be handled with compassion and finesse, as most people push back against the idea. If everyone loved and embraced it, they'd be doing it.

The fantastic news is that when you've gone as far as you can go with processes (you're never done and they're never perfect), you have virtually set yourself up to have an easier time setting up your company structure. Your processes will be forever in a cycle of iteration, but you're better off than you were without them.

KEY ACCELERANTS

→ *Be nimble.* You're not looking for perfection. If your process is perfect, it's probably about to be outdated.

→ *Standardize.* Scale is impossible without standardization and repeatability. Customization is the enemy.

→ *Design for the middle 60–70 percent.* That's how you accelerate.

→ *Document processes.* Don't allow for operations run by anecdotes.

→ *Be mindful of your speed.* Everyone's expecting you to make changes, but you have to do your due diligence, listen, and make the right ones.

→ *Promote a mindset of rapid iteration.* When you're scaling, the way you do things has to keep up with momentum and growth.

A by-product of landing your key accelerants is that they've clarified the roles you need. Not the people, but the roles. There's a big difference, and that's our next discussion.

CEO

MONTH: 6-9

MONTH: 4-6

MONTH: 1-4

STRUCTURE: FOCUS ON ROLES, NOT PEOPLE

A Cautionary Tale

Does this sound familiar?

A private equity-backed software company hires a new CEO to drive their new high-growth plan. The PE firm has underwritten a modest improvement in organic growth. As part of their diligence, they believe a new CEO who brings with them a proven commercial leader will be part of the answer. The PE firm trusts the CEO because he previously followed a founder-CEO and generated an exit that made the PE firm almost four times its money.

The CEO was able to do this in a market that was growing over 40 percent, and experienced a massive spike in demand due to COVID. The company thrived during a macro environment where underwriting rules for PE firms to acquire new portfolio companies were less strenuous. Meanwhile, the new company is in a low-double-digit-growth market and its competitive environment is more intense.

The customer base is ripe for cross-sell/upsell, but new customers are more difficult to find.

In the CEO's first forty-five days, he rightly identified that the sales function needed a new strategy. Unfortunately, he made the mistake many make. He brought his sales leader from the last business in to drive the change. This is a common misstep. Why? Because humans are nostalgic and like comfort. We love to reminisce about successes we've had with the team who made them possible. And no two strategies are the perfect match for two different companies. Not only that, but no two leadership teams are right for two different companies.

The CEO and the newly minted chief revenue officer (CRO) had done amazing things together in the past and trusted each other implicitly. The CEO gave his trusted friend a great deal of runway due to their past success and close relationship. He told the CRO to "do your thing."

Unfortunately, *his thing* wasn't *the thing* the business needed. After ten months in the seat, the CEO was forced to fire the CRO due to the common go-to-market issues I witnessed in these types of situations. The CEO lost credibility with the PE sponsor, executive management, and his good friend. The sales force felt the turnaround they faced was too formidable, with just over 40 percent of the top sellers leaving over a six-month mass exodus. (Note: The company had identified nineteen A-player representatives, and eight of them resigned during this time.) What's more, frontline sales management became disengaged. Most importantly, the search for the new CRO took almost six months.

By the time she landed in the role, the CEO had lost over one year of building the plan. At the time of this writing, the team is making slow progress on the way back up the mountain. The CEO is still in his role, but the time frame for the PE firm has been extended by almost two years due to this rush to "run the old playbook."

The CEO was so busy and had so much trust that he didn't notice what was happening, which was that the body rejected the organ. It wasn't just that the organization couldn't handle the rate of change; it was that the change wasn't connected to the overall strategy. Bringing someone in from your past isn't necessarily a bad thing, but it needs humility and clarity to be done well. Getting the band back together can be fun and it absolutely can work, as long as you're building your new thing together and not recreating the past.

Furthermore, as famously written by John Lydgate in 1440, "Comparisons are odious." Don't compare your last company to the new company. Decisions should always be based on the facts and the data of the company you're working with *now*.

There's a right way to switch up your organizational chart or bring on someone new. This chapter will show you how.

The What of Structure

Organizational structure is kind of like culture. Remember how culture is an emergent property that arises from having worked on purpose, vision, and values? Your appropriate organizational structure emerges from your strategy and processes. You know where you're going, and you have solid processes for getting there. In this chapter, I'll show you how your optimal organizational structure is likely right in front of you if you look at it the right way. You will need to make a change to the organization 100 percent of the time. The question is when and how significantly.

As the CEO, you should be designing the company to operate with velocity and without friction. So what's the smoothest way to establish structure? Get as objective as you can get. And the biggest obstacle to objectivity is *being a prisoner of the past.*

When many CEOs think about structure, they're thinking about who reports to whom. So they're thinking about the people. And the founder has set up who reports to whom in a way that, at the time, made perfect sense to them.

A founder-led business likely has established the primary functions: finance, sales, customer support/operations, product, and human capital. But they don't typically have discipline around the human capital part of the business, because their personal relationships dictate who does what. They don't lean into building a people function as quickly as they would a world-class sales function or a top-tier customer delivery function. The biggest issue probably isn't that you don't have the functions you need, it's that you don't have the right leadership and management structure for where the company needs to go next.

If you think about working with a charismatic, visionary leader, you can imagine that many people want to report to that person and have unfettered access to them. This widens the founder's span of control too much, meaning they have more than seven direct reports. Anyone with more than seven direct reports is going to have a problem sooner or later; they don't have enough time to devote to the active development of those individuals. As a consequence, there's a drag on velocity. When you have a velocity drag, employee and customer experience suffer. And these are your two most important stakeholders.

The Second CEO's job is to put individuals and their relationships aside for a moment and figure out what *roles* are required to activate the strategy. That's it. The most important mindset you can have right now is to get as close to objectivity as possible. Fortunately, there's a methodical way to evaluate what is and isn't working in your organizational structure. This sets you up to design the right structure to launch a new phase of clarity and momentum for the company. And because your processes are in better condition than when you arrived, you have a head start.

The How of Structure

The goal of sorting out structure is an organizational chart, right? But if you want to be successful at this as a Second CEO, don't start with the current chart. In fact, don't even look at it. This doesn't involve writing everyone's name on index cards and moving them around your desk in various configurations, bottom up. Would someone external do that? No. Someone *internal* would do that, led by their biases, relationships, history, and emotional baggage. Remember the first commandment for the Second CEO—think and act like you're from the outside.

Someone external would ask, *Do we have clearly defined functions, and do we have detailed processes for each function?*

Randy Street, former CEO of ghSMART who followed the founder, so aptly said: "With organizational design, you are looking to align priorities and the corresponding metrics with a leadership team that can execute against those with a high probability of success. As the CEO, always ask "Does this executive have a greater than 90 percent chance of performing in the top 10 percent for their respective role?" A question like this forces you to really look at the job to be done in the organizational structure and answer objectively."

Mapping It Out

As you go through your thinking around who reports to whom, there are a series of questions the Second CEO needs to ask. From the research for this book, my two decades of working with hundreds of companies, both public and PE-owned, here's a simple sequence to consider:

1. Where do we have unnecessary bottlenecks or balls being dropped that are impacting our ability to deliver for our clients/customers?

2. Why was the organizational chart set up in its current fashion? Be thorough in your discovery.

3. What's not getting done that should be getting done and why?

4. If we have a process, is it the execution of or the management of said process that's holding us back? Do we have a capability issue or a capacity issue? This is a simple way to frame the problem.

5. The immediate gaps must be shored up while you determine the longer-term, future-back organizational chart. Note: when you're in Horizon One (your first year), look to fill gaps in the current structure that are low-to-medium on disruption while you have an eye toward your future state organizational chart (three to five years out). Always be aware of what you are building toward.

6. As the CEO, how do you align the key metrics of a function with the key priorities of the business?

What Success Looks Like

You should feel you've succeeded when you can clearly articulate why the organizational structure is the way it is. Your reasons should be tied to customer satisfaction, employee engagement, and competitive advantage. The CEO has a primary responsibility to allocate human and financial capital to create value. You'll make changes; this is 100 percent certain. The depth of this first set of changes may not be where you go in Horizon Two, but that's OK. This is about making decisions in Year One to tackle current challenges to the best of your ability. Remember, change was never the point; the point was laying it all out so it makes sense to everyone and everyone knows what's expected of them.

Troubleshooting
THE DEVIL IS IN THE DETAILS

Sometimes mapping out your structure is simple, and sometimes it's not. Here's a variety of circumstances where it's not so simple, and how to handle them.

You have bottlenecks you can't figure out, and they're leading to customer dissatisfaction.

There are almost always three possible reasons for bottlenecks:

1. You don't have a process to deliver value (or you do and it's broken).

2. You have the wrong people running the process.

3. You have a combination of both.

The Second CEO needs to assess the situation, determine if they have a process problem, a people problem, or both, and then venture to *answer the right question.*

If you're certain you have a *process* problem, refer back to chapter 7 for how to fix the process and/or build the right processes that are scalable so the team can execute.

If you have a process and it's not getting executed correctly, then you have a *people* problem. It's usually a leadership problem, because the leader isn't assuming accountability around that process. The role of the leader for each process should be clear to everyone, and each leader's scorecard should lay out precisely which processes they own, along with the appropriate metrics. Assuming you've got the scorecard and the issue is that the leader is subpar, you're either coaching them up or exiting them.

Meanwhile, sometimes things are a bit murkier, and you might have the right person but they need some coaching for their gaps *and* the methodology to run their function is wrong. In this case, fix your process first, and make sure the roles and direct reports are set up in a manner to drive velocity without friction. From here, you can reassess your person against the scorecard.

SOMEONE'S SPAN OF CONTROL IS TOO WIDE

Some companies were operating with more than seven people reporting to one person and only a few reporting to another, and the why of that came down to personalities and preferences. No one complained; they liked it that way. And when you're a small organization, you can get away with that for a while. But no one person can lead their function while also developing more than seven people. You're going to have to break a little glass on the issue of who reports to whom.

Ruffling feathers is unavoidable, but you can present your changes to the employees in an empathetic and clear way. It's all about transparency and pulling your trusted A-players into the tent. Let them know you're making some changes, and why. Solicit feedback from those trusted people about how to communicate to the employee base in a way they will best receive the information. Ask what questions the employees are likely to have, map out your responses, and lay out what you're going to do and why. And be brutally honest, including saying:

I don't know if this is the perfect structure. What I do know, based on the evidence, is that we need to make these changes to get to the next milestone and to our vision of who we said we want to be. And I'm ultimately accountable to make those changes. So give me some grace, because some of these changes may not be right. But I promise to communicate with you throughout on how we're doing and the indicators I'm using to judge success.

—*The Second CEO*

YOU'RE WEIGHTING THE OPINIONS OF THOSE AROUND YOU TOO HEAVILY

Someone says, "I've been talking to the founder about so and so reporting to me and why that makes sense." There's a tendency to cave and listen to the internal team on who should report to whom. Unfortunately, that's the wrong strategy, period. Not to mention this particular example involves the founder, and the whole point of your position is to do for the company what the founder wasn't able to do. You need to take an objective view of what the company needs to scale, and what sort of capabilities are required to make a certain function operate at a high level.

THE LAND GRAB

There might be employees looking for a land grab when there's a change in leadership. They want to flex their muscles and expand their span of control. You need to guard against this by thanking them for their input and then moving on. Everybody gets a voice, but not everybody gets a vote.

The Artistry of Change

The Second CEO is in a position where they're expected to make changes to organizational structure. But not for the sake of change, not too soon or too late, and not because they're chasing security or certainty. There's an artistry to it, but that artistry comes only after the fundamentals are present. Here are some tips:

- Try to be more evolutionary than revolutionary. Don't make dramatic changes in the first 180 days, unless they're necessary. For example, if you're going into a situation where you already know there's a toxic culture, and there's a person or two—even on the management team—who's the source, you make that change quickly. Don't let a known toxic person stick around.

- The Listening Tour isn't just a vehicle for gathering information, and it doesn't stop after ninety days. You should always be listening more than you're talking.

- The employees need you to show them what kind of a leader you are in the first year, and you do that by managing change. All of your changes should make sense and map onto the strategy you've laid out to increase momentum and growth to get to where you want to be in five years. And you should communicate all of the changes in an empathetic way and take the time to be certain everyone understands what you're doing and why.

- Don't insist on having all possible information before you make a decision. Part of being a great decision-maker is not being attached to having all the information you think you need. You're looking to clear the 75 percent hurdle of information. Don't wait or go searching for more than 75 percent.

- Have a flexible mindset. Be prepared to have to make changes after you make some decisions. No one gets every decision right. If you don't like a decision you make six months from now, reverse it with transparency. Document the mistake you made or the assumptions you had that were wrong so that you learn how to be a better decision-maker going forward in the company.

Once you have your organizational structure and you're able to add the names of the leaders, whether they're A-players now or you've set them on their way, you have to answer a question many ignore: *What happens if they leave?* In the next chapter, I'll discuss developing a robust and deep team beyond the C-suite.

KEY ACCELERANTS

→ Base decisions on the facts and the data of the company you're working with *now*, not on one you worked with in the past.

→ Embrace the idea of making changes in the first year. Everyone's expecting you to.

→ Lean into the people function with all you've got. If it's not part of the Executive team, change that.

→ Put individuals and their relationships aside for a moment, and figure out what *roles* are required to activate the strategy.

→ Think like an external hire.

→ Using scorecards for each position will help keep your work focused on what's best for the role.

CEO

MONTH: 6-9

MONTH: 4-6

MONTH: 1-4

BUILDING YOUR TEAM

We specialize in founder-based businesses. Our underwriting criteria has six major categories. The first one is team, and it's the first one for a reason. We are looking for a partner in addition to a price. I'd rather see us pay a little more for the business that has a great team than people we can't work with, even if they have a great business. Getting the team right is paramount for us.

TOM MCKELVEY, *Cofounder, Gauge Capital*

You've spent at least six months understanding the marketplace, understanding how the company runs internally, and thinking through organizational change. Now it's time for one of the most important parts of your first-year journey: selecting your team.

When you're following a founder, there's always a tendency to hang onto historical, legacy rituals that exist in a business. And that can do wonders for morale if the culture was healthy and positive. The same can be true for hanging onto people. And while it might be true that everyone loved the C-suite, you have to ask yourself,

Knowing what I now know, how do I determine if these wonderful folks who worked well alongside the founder are also my *people?*

This chapter will help you answer that question, and it'll also help you build a different team, if that's what you need, with a three-step process:

- Understand who you have.

- Identify what you need.

- Create a cohesive and well-functioning team.

Understand Who You Have

As the Second CEO, whether you're from the outside or not, you must objectively assess the talent you have. Ideally, you'll be inspecting the performance management standards and performance reviews. Specifically, you're looking for whether they use any sort of a forced ranking, where there's a clear sign of who the A-, B-, and C-players are. But that's not always available or in that form, so I'll describe my process for getting that part up to speed.

As always, you want to be transparent and communicate your intentions.

Part of my process over the next one-to-two quarters is to deeply understand a series of things, including how we manage people. One of the things that allows me to do that, is reading through the history of our performance management process. So I'm asking our head of HR to send me this year's performance reviews, last year's, a scatterplot of the A-, B-, and C-players, and how we aggregate human capital.

—The Second CEO

The reason this first step is imperative is it also tells you something about culture. If you don't have a robust performance process, how does any manager, whether executive or front line, drive performance? Furthermore, how do they activate the B-players who have the potential to be As? Reading the performance reviews of your direct reports and their direct reports will give you a sense of the leadership ethos as well as the people-ethos of the company. Armed with this, you can look objectively at the executive team and any available reviews.

As you read this you might be saying, "Well, that is a no-brainer." It is, but the consistency with which this happens in the two decades of observing founder-led businesses is low. Human beings lack self-awareness and objectivity when it comes to ranking their own performance. And we all have short-term memories when asked to reflect on our annual performance. To perpetuate a high-performance culture, you must document an individual's performance.

Let them see the words, their ratings, and their developmental items. This ensures that the people leaders are thoughtful in their approach, which improves the employee experience. This also ensures the employees have complete clarity on where they stand. And because performance reviews determine bonus payouts and promotion opportunities, this level of rigor normalizes why people get or don't get the opportunities and the dollars they covet.

The final chunk of data at your disposal is the past six months. You've had ample time to assess your leadership team, both directly and indirectly. People have explained their roles to you, offered their opinions on purpose, vision, and values, and told you about the core processes that run their function. You've been able to get feedback from clients, too. So you now have a full picture of the team you've inherited—not only from subjective measures but also from objective measures. What do you do with all this?

THE FIRST ROLE TO ASSESS

Part of your job as a CEO is to build a culture of high performance, so a top-notch people function is crucial. Remember that most Second CEOs will be developing that function for the first time because founders tend to be more intuitive and less systematic. This is the time to ask yourself, *Do I have the right chief people officer?* When you have the right people leader, everything else is easier.

You know you might have the right people leader if that person has a robust system for reviewing performance that's methodical and structured. It should be at least semiannual and annual, and give you the insight you need about gaps. This is a necessary foundation. Just as nonnegotiable, however, is that your people leader can work as a team member and leader, elevating the performance of the team with everything they say and do. If you have that, determining what you have in the rest of the team is likely to be smooth.

My only caveat here is that understanding who you have also includes their level of commitment to the company's vision and core values. Is your current chief people officer a shining beacon of the company's values? Of all positions, your people leader must embody the culture. As CEO, you are the head of culture and your chief people officer is right alongside you.

If you don't have what you need in your people leader and their gaps can't be filled in eighteen months, start your search for a replacement with an outside firm. *Why?* Because you're going to get better impact and better focus. Your internal recruiting team has the ability, but at the C-suite level, going with a professional search firm sends a message to new candidates that you're investing in talent. You're building this business the right way. This doesn't mean you don't also post the position internally. You're signaling that when it comes to people decisions, you're exhaustive and will not succumb to internal pressure to always promote from within. This is part of building *your* team versus *the* team.

When you do a search, you're forced to make certain you understand how to pitch the company's value proposition and strategy to people on the outside. You must be able to do this anyway, because attracting talent is a top-tier responsibility of the CEO. You're the number one recruiter in the company.

In addition, you'll learn from outside candidates. There are things you're not thinking about that they'll mention, such as perspectives on your company that *even with you coming in from the outside* you weren't aware of. You're going to gain invaluable strategic insight from launching this process.

Finally, you're going to see your company in action. How a company hires and onboards senior talent is oftentimes a key determining factor in your ability to attract the right people. They need to be blown away by the opportunity and the people they meet when they're going through an interview process.

THE REST OF THE EXECUTIVE TEAM

From the Listening Tour to asking your leaders to document their processes to observing how they work as members of a team, you're collecting clues to who each person is and how they operate. If you don't already know the answers to the following questions, now's the time to schedule one-on-ones.

- Walk me through how you run your function.

- What's going well?

- What's not working?

- What are the key processes your team follows?

- How are you building and scaling?

- What do you need to be successful?

If a leader lays out structured, thoughtful answers to these questions, at the very least you know they're a strong contender to remain in their position.

JUST A CONTENDER?

Knowing someone is capable as an individual contributor is a solid start. But you also need a sense of their capability as a leader and developer of other A-players. You might have an individual superstar on your hands, but what you really need is someone who can grow and scale their function while being a team player as well as a leader.

Similarly, there are superstars who get good results the wrong way. Maybe you've heard rumblings about people not trusting them. If you have a set of values in the company that someone is violating, as my coach Tim Stratman says, "that's the most dangerous person you've got." And usually that person needs to go. He continues,

> "They're not leaders; they're performers. They might be outstanding individual contributors, but they never made the transition to leader. And when you confront them, they say, *Well, look at my scorecard!* But their scorecard isn't the one that matters. It's the team scorecard that matters."

Ultimately, understanding who you have is like giving you a picture of the past, and you also need to know if they're committed and capable of walking with you into the future.

CHECK ON COMMITMENT

You have to handle commitment head-on.

Are you committed to this next chapter? No harm, no foul if you're not. I'm happy to figure out a mutually beneficial way for you to depart. Maybe it's time to explore you doing something else in the company that's the highest and best use of your time?

—*The Second CEO*

At the start of your tenure, everyone's on their best behavior, and if you asked this question then, you'd hear a lot of proclamations of unwavering commitment. We can all put on our best face for a week or two, or even a month. But it's safe to say you've officially had enough time to see how everyone shows up, in real time. You should have a pretty strong thesis about who's on your team and who's not.

You might be asking, *What if they say they're all-in, but they've been in the C-suite for a handful of years and they'd like to downshift and do something else?*

I think that's a great sign of high self-awareness. Here's my caution: You'd essentially be demoting someone and putting them into a role where they can be their best, that's not a parking lot for them to quietly look for a job and collect a paycheck. You have to ask yourself, *Is this just postponing the inevitable, or are they truly committed to this role?* Maybe it was an example of the Peter Principle, where they were promoted one level above where they should have been and should have never been in the C-suite. Who knows what the real story is?

But what I do know, from experience, is that greater than 90 percent of the time, demoting somebody from the C-suite doesn't work. My recommendation is always that it's time for that person to go, for cultural reasons. It's time for them to reach their full potential somewhere else, and you should celebrate their contributions to the business. It shouldn't be a negative experience. It should be a positive one, because you're now also unlocking an opportunity to promote or go external and make a better match for the scorecard of that position.

Identify Who You Need

Once you have a picture of the past and the present, it's time to identify who you need for the future. We'll begin, as we usually do, with making sure you have a scorecard and a vision of what each person in the C-suite needs to drive the future strategy.

Remember that you construct scorecards as a future-back thinker. *For you to achieve your five-year plan, what does each function need to do and what does the person leading that function need to have?* Scorecards in hand, you can objectively compare the scorecard for, say, the CFO, to the current CFO. You can assess the CFO for gaps and for how close they are to a 100 percent match with the scorecard. Were they a great fit for the job in the past, doing well now, and also capable of leading into the future? You decide.

You may say, "I'm not sure what I need the future of each role to look like." This is a mistake. As the CEO, you must have a clear vision of the three- to five-year strategy by now and, as part of this, the capabilities needed in each role. This is where external help can be of the highest value. Work with a leadership firm to help you define your future state. Then take this thinking to your board and mentors/peers and bounce it off of them. As the CEO, you have three central responsibilities:

1. Culture

2. Vision/Strategy

3. Team

You cannot afford to shortchange this process; however, many do as we are often in a rush to get roles filled and keep the trains moving.

The scorecard is a bridge from the past to the future.

Create a Cohesive, Well-Functioning Team

I've seen many CEOs assemble superstars who have stellar capabilities running their functions. That's only part of what you need. Your functional leaders need to operate as a cohesive team. They need to have the ability to put their egos aside and work for the greater good. It's similar to a sports franchise that signs a number of high-priced free agents, but they all want the limelight. If nobody wants to share the credit, that's not conducive to team building.

You're evaluating and building your team with A-player functional abilities who can attract, develop, and retain employees that have the potential to be better than them. That last part will be the single greatest differentiator between you meeting your objectives and exceeding them. A well-aligned team is the 10x factor for achieving outcomes. You're looking for people who have a history of developing others. You're looking for people who say *we* not *I*.

You want executives who worry about the good of the company, not their individual pay plan and promotion path. You can always tell when somebody has successfully transitioned to a true executive: They start all of their sentences with "The team may need" or "The team has expressed" versus saying "I think" or "I need." Executives have a long-term view: they think about the achievement of the five-year strategy, not maximizing in-year income. Be very wary of those who operate in the latter sphere.

A mistake many Second CEOs make—and that includes me—is looking at individual C-suite folks, deciding someone is the right person to run the function, and underestimating the importance of how that person works cross-functionally. Your C-suite should work well not only with other members of the C-team but also with other members of the organization.

Is there a way to ensure you have someone who can work that way? Yes. Step one is assessing each member of the C-suite to make sure they aren't all wired the same way. I'm not going to promote any one evaluation tool as I see the value in analyzing people from different angles.

Whether you use StrengthsFinder, Kolbe, or DISC when you're team building, pick a tool you know or hire somebody who does this for a living. You don't want a team of people who are similar in their strengths, what they're drawn to, the way they prefer to relate, and how they're wired to handle information or conflict. That's the one thing all these systems have in common: make sure you have a well-rounded mix of "types."

It's a delicate balance, I know, because it can be tempting to fill your C-suite with skillful leaders who are functional superstars. But if they don't play well with one another, you've volunteered for a job you don't want: referee.

I had a client who was a big fan of using DISC profiles. What they recognized is if everybody on the team was high in D (i.e., dominant, high initiative, and super competitive), you're going to have a driven, proactive team, but there's going to be glass getting broken everywhere. And probably some sharp elbows being flung around. You need a balance of Dominance, Influence, Steadiness, and Conscientiousness to ensure chemistry across the team.

AGAIN, HERE'S TIM STRATMAN . . .

The leader has to achieve through other people, and their first critical group of other people is the executive leadership team. They're only going to be as good as you are. So if you aren't leading by example, none of this works. And you all have to be aligned on values and strategy. And you have to trust each other enough to have the hard conversations, question each other, and have the kind of active debate that creates better choices.

For leaders, at the end of the day, it's behavior that wins or loses the battle. Do I listen to alternative opinions? Am I open to the feedback of other people? Do I solicit feedback prior to making decisions? Does my team have each others' backs? Or is this a political minefield, where we say one thing in the room and then we say something else outside the room, which is pretty typical, unfortunately. Teamwork is so important that I'll always bet on the team that works well together and executes well over the one with superb strategy.

I look at this as an organism, and we want it to be as healthy as possible. So no egos. Ego will absolutely tank you as a leader. And address or root out any toxicity in the team and the culture. And make sure you can point to people living the values.

It's not unusual for a CEO to tell me, "We've been talking about the four cultural pillars for decades. We've been talking about the strategy, everybody's got that." And then I'll ask questions, and we'll find out they don't.

A fantastic example of a Second CEO following a methodical people process to rebuild a team is Eric Walczykowski from Bespoke Partners. In chapter 1, I introduced him and Kristie Nova, the founder he followed. You may recall Eric was hired to come in as president for a year of transition before stepping into CEO.

Eric's conversations and observations pointed him to three critical changes necessary to activate the vision he and Kristie had for Bespoke:

1. They needed to professionalize finance and operations to get better at running a people-based business with better margin control and better utilization. He knew he needed someone who understood offshore resources, and he launched a search and found somebody who turned out to be an A-player and who's thriving in their role.

2. He recognized they needed to upskill the people function from a director level of HR to a true chief people officer. After all, the business is a search firm and is dependent on people. Eric went out into the market and brought in an experienced chief people officer who had been part of multiple transition transformations in both large and smaller companies. This person had the ability to significantly upskill the collective maturity of the leaders, including by being a mentor to many of the younger partners who happen to be female. Eric hired a woman because he knew the leadership team needed more diversity.

3. Eric identified a gap in the leadership team with his move up to CEO. There needed to be a real Number Two who could leave the commercial/sales function. And while it was taking longer than he wanted to find that person, Eric went outside and got an interim consultant to bring scale and replication to the team while looking for the right candidate. He found the right person, his chief commercial officer, who, at the time of this writing, is about to be finalized. Eric has been beyond judicious in making sure he has the right one.

The How and When of Working as a Team

THE EXECUTIVE TEAM'S OPERATING PRINCIPLES AND OPERATING CADENCE

As the CEO, you need to establish ground rules and a framework for what a high-performing team looks like as well as cadence for your work together.

OPERATING PRINCIPLES

Operating principles govern how you work as a team. Typically, an executive team would have no more than five operating principles. Examples of operating principles include:

- *We always act with positive intent and assume positive intent.* This principle means you're giving the benefit of the doubt even when you're getting critical feedback.

- *Nobody has all of the answers, but together we can have all of the answers.* This is an example of focusing on *what's* right, not *who's* right, and always putting the greater good of the team and the organization in front of your own.

- *Collectively own decisions.* While you might have disagreed behind closed doors in a meeting, and you might have been out-voted on an initiative, when you come out of that meeting, you all collectively own that decision. You don't say, "Well, I'm not really on board with this. I got out-voted." Can you put the team above yourself and be part of a unified front?

As you come up with your operating principles with the team, look at each individual and ask yourself, *Does this person adhere to these and do they operate consistently according to the principles?* This question can be the basis of your team development plan.

OPERATING CADENCE

Every CEO needs to establish operating norms. These are rhythms and expectations that nudge average performers to above-average levels and make good performers great. Here are some examples of critical parts of your cadence:

1. A *daily* huddle, in small teams. This is one of the most powerful operating norms that Second CEOs can put in place. It allows for rapid problem-solving as well as rapid sharing of what's working in the business. It should include the following, and you'll customize according to your needs:

    a. Each person lays out what their goals are for the day.

    b. They each name the most important thing they want to get done.

    c. They share some good news from the day before.

    d. Talk about an item that they're stuck with or struggling with.

    e. Update on one of their quarterly goals.

2. A *weekly* staff meeting. This is how you build a high-functioning, high-velocity organization. Regardless of which operating or management method you're using to run the firm, weekly meetings with your direct reports are nonnegotiable. Report on things that are working, as well as one or two obstacles that are getting in the way of the business.

3. A *weekly* all-hands call. During COVID, we saw a lot of companies move from a monthly or quarterly all-hands call with all employees to doing things more frequently. However, this was something the Second CEOs we work with had been doing well before COVID.

   The purpose of communicating with the team even for fifteen minutes a week is velocity, transparency, and continuing to lay out the vision of why you're doing what you're doing. And remember that the moment you think you're done speaking to the team and reminding them where you're going is the moment you need to say it again. Repetition is key.

4. A *monthly* call with your private equity firm (and most will ask for one) where you review the financials. This is a smaller group, usually your CFO, you, and the key people from the private equity firm. Most times this doesn't involve independent board members.

   Also, this is a great opportunity for you to share with the private equity firm where you're seeing things bubbling up in the business as well as where you're seeing opportunity. When you take money from somebody from an investment perspective, the financial rigor in the business increases. You should expect this level of scrutiny.

5. *Quarterly* meetings. Over the past two-and-a-half decades, I've been able to observe all sorts of quarterly rhythms. Here are my best practices:

   □ The CEO should meet with the executive leadership team on week nine or ten of each quarter. The topics of this meeting should be: *what's getting in the way, where are our biggest obstacles or opportunities?* And then the team problem-solves together. You should have a list of two to four things that you bring to your board meeting, which should be on week twelve or thirteen of the quarter. The board should help you problem-solve.

▫ The CEO should meet with the board quarterly. One quarter the meeting can be done virtually, and the next quarter it should be done in person. The virtual meeting can be more of a tactical operating meeting that involves a little more near-term problem-solving, and the in-person meeting is the opportunity for the CEO to lay out some key strategic gaps that they have. It's the time to get the best minds around these big strategic issues and ensure that the board is aligned with the direction of the company. Plus, it's always good to have a board dinner, some social time, and ensure you have the right chemistry with your board. You may choose to do all in-person board meetings in your first year, which makes sense. Use this as an operating guide, not a mandate.

Measuring Performance

A must for every CEO is to have your C-suite rank how the team is performing. You do this by laying out each individual operating principle a couple of weeks before your quarterly business review. Everybody is required to assess, on a scale of one to five, how they believe the team is operating. That feedback bubbles up to you, and it's incumbent upon you to spend time at the leadership meeting discussing how you're doing as a team.

This is what you guys said we're doing. You think we're a three out of five on this principle, five on this, a two on that. Let's talk about it.

As a team, you identify one or two key bottlenecks and agree to resolve them in the next quarter. This rhythm of reviewing how you're performing as a team each quarter, along with then shifting to talking about how the business is doing, is your process of continuous improvement.

You're balancing the two components: team and company. And you're continuing to model the behavior you want your leaders to model with their teams, always investing in how you improve as a team. *How do we become more high performance?* is your driving question. You should always be modeling the prioritization of team cohesion and team chemistry over anything else.

Common Missteps

- *Moving too slowly.* Taking too much time to move the people out who you know don't have the skill set they need.

- *Hanging onto people* because you don't want to be too disruptive in your first year. The organization is expecting change; they're ready for you to make change. And you shouldn't waste the opportunity to create new momentum and bring in fresh blood.

- *Bringing people in from your previous life* whom you trust and have comfort with but who don't match the scorecard and the culture. Don't expedite your hiring process by grabbing your security blanket from your past job. Instead, hire a search firm, build a scorecard, and see what the market gives you. And while it's less efficient in the short term, it's more effective in the long run.

- *Taking feedback from others.* "So-and-so needs to go!" There's natural positioning and manipulation of the Second CEO because people want to move their own agenda forward. Be judicious.

- *Defaulting to internal promotions.* If you're replacing three or four people on your leadership team over the first twelve months, you want equal parts internal promotion and external search. This brings the right balance to the formation of a new team.

KEY ACCELERANTS

→ Understanding who you have. And you won't be able to until you have a robust performance process.

→ A chief people leader who embodies the culture.

→ A head of HR isn't enough. If you don't have a chief people leader you're sending a message that people aren't as important as other functions.

→ Identify what you need. *What does each function need to do and what does the person leading that function need to have?* Break out your scorecards!

→ Create a cohesive and well-functioning team. A well-aligned team is the 10x factor for achieving outcomes. Remember that leaders achieve through other people. You're looking for people who have a history of developing others.

→ Put your energy into identifying high performers who can work cross-functionally and as a team. Many superstars are high performers who might be liabilities. Keep your eye on the whole package and not just high performance.

BUILDING YOUR TWO BOARDS

Part of being able to accelerate and scale the way you need to is surrounding yourself with the right advisors. You're leading the business with a Two-Horizon approach. In your mind, you're considering the near-term, first-year objectives, as well as the longer-term more strategic ones. To improve your probability of success, you must surround yourself with the right advisors. Looking back, one of the best things I did as a CEO was build my personal board along with the formal, fiduciary board of directors for the company. Let me explain the difference.

Your Board

When you get to the top, the information flow decreases, it doesn't increase. People talk to you less candidly when you're at the top because of the implication of your power position. You're not going to the board to talk to them about that. You have to be very careful about what you share and how you share it.

MY COACH, TIM STRATMAN

Moving forward, the key ingredient to the continuation of your success is the people advising you. You cannot do this alone. No one can. We don't see our blind spots, by definition. You need to assemble your dream team:

1. *A coach.* Yes, you need one. Congratulations if you've made it this far without one. Really. Kudos. What separates extraordinary leaders from the pack, though, is that they have a coach. And forgive the analogy, but I need to make a point. If the greatest athletes in the world have multiple coaches, how can you operate without one? To be a one-percenter, you must have one-percenter habits.

2. *Mentor(s).* These are CEOs who've been there and done that and can support you. They've done what you're attempting to do and can help guide you. You should be able to contact them about the day-to-day tactical questions, as well as the more strategic ones. They're available to you and generous with their time and wisdom.

3. *Peers.* These are new CEOs like you. They're at similar stages/industries and have a mandate like you. They're working in founder-based environments. You can compare notes and experiences, and travel this unique road together.

The Company's Board

Realistically, many founder-owned businesses don't have a formal board of directors. And if you're walking into a company without a board, create one and run the company like it's private equity backed.

One of the values of private equity–backed companies is there's a defined operating rhythm they expect from their portfolio companies. They believe in quarterly board meetings to talk about initiatives; monthly financial reviews; discussions with lenders to ensure that the company is being properly managed; and healthy governance practices. That kind of structure helps everyone. If you're not required to have it, do it anyway.

Many reading this book are part of private equity–backed companies and will have some composition of a board. My intention here is to lay out how to build the right board. What's the "right board?" A great board allows you and the executive team a higher probability of accomplishing your strategic objectives in less time while avoiding common pitfalls. They are amazing advisors who have seen it and done it.

How to Build a Fiduciary Board

1. Work with your investors or your executive team to identify your top three most important items for creating outsized value (i.e., your VCP).

2. Recognize that there are typically five roles you can have on a board, and pick the two or three that are most important to achieving your objectives in the VCP. The roles are:

    a. *CEO whisperer/coach.* This person has been there and done it.

    b. *VOC—voice of customer.* This board member can speak to selling into a particular segment/customer and knows them intimately.

   c. *Functional depth.* This board member brings specific functional depth to your firm for a critical area. For example, you may be attempting to productize your traditional project-based offerings. Having somebody deep in technology/productization on your board is critical.

   d. *Industry depth.* This board member understands a key industry/segment that you're selling into. This may be a new industry you're expanding into and you need this as part of your VCP.

   e. *Capital-structure depth.* This board member knows how to shift from being private to going public. Or maybe you're getting ready to do a series of acquisitions. From sourcing to diligence to integration, this board member has done it before and knows how to manage the natural speedbumps.

3. For each of those levers or initiatives, there's an expert somewhere who can serve as an advisor on your board. You're going to find those three people and ask them to be on your board.

Why three? In my experience, you want no more than three independent directors because you want good, objective counsel to sit alongside the financial sponsor on your board. You also want a board that will reach down and work, side by side, with your executive team. This will make for good advice and good debate, without the bureaucracy that can slow things down and/or be overwhelming.

4. Define your expectations. *What am I asking these people to do, exactly?* This is the most common question right about now. *How do I know what a good board member looks like? How often do I speak to them?* Defining a board member is just like defining any other role in the company. You need to have a scorecard for what that board member will do.

In the research for this book, and in running SBI, I've found the priority should be what I call *active board effectiveness.* An active board member doesn't just show up at the board meeting every ninety days, ask three big questions, and then go away. Effective boards operate as a team, and they also operate between board meetings. This is where the value gets delivered by your board members.

Remember that every CEO should have a board member who's a CEO coach/CEO whisperer. This is a person who has seen it and done it and can be an advocate and sounding board as you navigate all the challenges of being a CEO. Some people opt to have a board member play this role. Some people, like myself, opt to have a CEO coach like Tim Stratman, who's not on the board.

I was blessed to have Jacob Silverman, CEO of Kroll, on the SBI board. He was and continues to be an incredible sounding board and advisor to me and SBI. Jake knows the journey of scaling a professional services firm through multiple stages of growth with a variety of PE sponsors. He was perfect for us. You want someone who has the situational awareness of the scenario you're in, and who also has a track record of having accomplished the very thing you're looking to accomplish with the business over the next three to five years. Do they have a track record of helping other CEOs become great?

This person may or may not still be in an operating role elsewhere. What matters is how you fit with them and how you can work with them. So take a very strong opinion with your lead investor on this archetype, and hire a search firm to find someone who can play that role. The key quality of great board members is they're independent. They're not operating partners who work for the private equity firm.

The other two board roles for your independent board represent the areas of value creation that are most important or have the most risk attached to you pulling them off. For example, you may be moving into a new market, selling to a new buyer, and you don't have a lot of familiarity with what that looks like. Finding a board member who understands that market segment, those buyers, and which products or services get consumed well in that segment and which ones don't, is critical. So this board member would be considered your VOC/functional board member.

Finally, there are the personal qualities. You want people who are passionate about what you do. They *want* to be coaches and advisors; they don't want to operate. And they need to be comfortable working with your broader leadership team. Having an active board means you have board members who are interfacing directly with your C-suite on a regular basis. This gives you operating leverage and it also provides great mentorship for the people on your direct team.

Judge your board members on what they do between the board meetings, not at the board meetings. *What do I mean?* Active board effectiveness. A great board member is in a natural cadence in their area of specialty with the leadership team. When you look back on a quarter, you can point to specific areas where their counsel and support was helpful. They opened new doors to acquire a customer. They participated in a working session to solve a problem. They helped recruit a new A-player senior hire. They introduced a new channel partner. Judge board members on both strategic work and in the flow support.

5. Choose a leader. While you're constructing the board, think about who's going to lead it and help them become a team. Typically, you'll be choosing one of your three independent people for this role.

   You'll compensate this person a little bit more than you would your traditional board members, and their role is to work directly with you on the formation of the board agenda. This person needs to make sure board meetings are effective and that the board operates as a team, not independent franchise advisors who swoop in and swoop out. It's part of that person's job to make sure that happens.

   The way I've seen this work best is this lead director typically would have a cadence with the board where they would have a board-only call at the halfway point of the quarter. This is a call you as CEO are not attending. You lean on your lead director to drive this. They give quick updates on what's happening with the business, talk about key initiatives and things they're observing with the other members on the board, which then help you as the CEO shape your upcoming board agenda. They also can provide a bit of a buffer with the PE/financial sponsor due to their credibility.

6. Help the founder move forward. I recently spoke with Brian Ruder, Partner and Co.'s Head of Technology Investing of top-tier private equity firm Permira, and Bruce Chizen, former CEO of Adobe, who followed the founder. They both mentioned the founder will likely still be on the board. Depending on your relationship and how well the handoff was architected, that might be wonderful. But even if it is, the founder should step off the board after a year. *Why?*

   □ They tend to be too attached to the past.

   □ They slow down decision-making rather than accelerate it if their priority is their legacy.

   □ They delay the Second CEO's ability to assemble *their* team. As Brian said, "There's too much defaulting to them, and you don't get the space you need."

I think it's important for the management team to play a leading role in bringing on independent board members. I find it helpful to bring in voices and views that are independent of the typical financial sponsor perspective. We were able to bring on three terrific independent board members who bring different attributes, skill sets and experiences. They don't control the board, but they have a voice, and that can be very meaningful in terms of advancing the discussion.

We're looking for dimensions that can bring a unique perspective, capability, new relationships and diversity that we might not be getting from our sponsors—all in the interest of governing and value-creating as effectively as possible.

JAKE SILVERMAN, CEO, Kroll

Crafting Effective Board Meetings

The job of your board is to help the executive leadership team remove the biggest strategic obstacles holding you back from achieving your ultimate vision. *How do you best do that?* Probably not by spending an inordinate amount of time preparing slides and detailed information that never gets covered. But you can spend some time strategically preparing a presentation that gets the job done and removes obstacles.

The first slide of the board deck should be the agenda for the meeting, and it should go out at least a week in advance. This slide presents three or four items the executive team is looking for board feedback on. This way, everyone is showing up with a context and with ideas. They're already thinking critically about the agenda items and how they might be of help.

The agenda, in other words, is about removing these obstacles—not going through financial details. The latter happens in the monthly financial cadence with your lead investor, which is a different meeting. Yes, it's important to know the financials, and you need to know where you're at. But that's not the function of the board meeting. Instead, it's an opportunity to put a handful of amazing brains in a room to help you gain clarity on how to clear your path and accomplish your objectives.

Lastly, I'm a believer in action and 100 percent participation. No one is just sitting on the sidelines. And that includes board members, who both assign action items and have action items to complete. Any board member who's not willing to invest their own money and time alongside you, as part of the VCP, isn't a board member you want. There isn't universal consensus on this; it's my informed opinion.

Boards that work best are composed of people who truly believe in the business and are willing to invest alongside you. And they get to participate in the upside as a result. The compensation for these board members should have three components:

1. An investment that they put in at the same class of stock as you and the private equity firm.

2. An annual retainer of somewhere between $30,000 and $100,000 a year. The amount depends on level of experience, size of your company, and how you package their total compensation for the role (i.e., cash versus equity).

3. A gifted percentage of equity for their time and their strategic advice. This is the best operating construct I've seen. Building an effective board includes having aligned incentives.

Brandon Nixon is a Second CEO who followed the founder at Lytx. Lytx is an industry-leading technology company specializing in video telematics used by commercial and public fleet vehicles. It has become an incredibly successful PE-backed company scaling from a small business to a multibillion-dollar enterprise and industry leader. Brandon builds his board with an eye on strategic support. His advice? "Build a board that is intellectually curious. Often, board members simply give advice on how to run your business. But, I find it far more valuable when the board engages with intellectual curiosity about our industry and our business strategies, and they ask questions testing our thinking and decisions. Doing so, makes us better."

Your Relationship with the Board

Priority one is to immediately develop relationships with everyone on the existing board. Invest that time; it's necessary. If you inherited a board, at about nine months in, when the critical Horizon One tasks have been handled, it's time to be objective about whether there are board members who need to leave. You don't want to wait two years to replace a board member if there's an area you need help with that isn't represented on the board.

You only know someone isn't right if you're constantly communicating with the board members and you know what their strengths are. There's no such thing as too much communication with the board, and that includes all kinds of news. If you have bad news or you're off plan, don't run away or go dark. Bad news doesn't get any better with time. When things go sideways, your board is there to help you, not judge you. As Investcorp's Dave Tayeh (Head of North American Private Equity) says, "There's one table and it's round. Your investors and board members are on your side." Use your board members and communicate with them frequently.

Dave also urges you to be open-minded. "If your mind is closed, you'll miss things. I know you want to show that you've got it and it's all under control, but that's counterproductive. Your team and your board are going to lose faith in you if they see you're not being honest and open about when you need help."

The Second CEO's relationship with the board is a vital component of their success. It needs to be nurtured and maintained, and at all times transparent. As far as meetings go, as discussed in chapter 8, the ideal board cadence is once a quarter virtually and once a quarter in person. Your goal is to be surrounded by the best minds available for the strategic issues that are critical for your Horizon Two.

KEY ACCELERANTS

→ There are few things more important than having your own personal board. Second CEOs who go into the job with that, in my experience, outperform the rest.

→ You only need three independent board members, but they need to be the right people. They need to be amazing at exactly what you need.

→ Use board meeting time wisely. Don't go through the minutiae of the financials. You're with the people best positioned to help you with big, strategic issues. Pick their brains!

→ The board is on your side. Making it adversarial is inappropriate and not a good use of everyone's valuable time. Communicate with them frequently, and be as open as possible, including about things that aren't going well.

CONCLUSION

Reaching Your Full Potential as Second CEO

Enjoying the Journey

My original intention for writing this book was to make life as a Second CEO better and more enjoyable. You're not the first one to be in this position. And now you have a book filled with advice from some of the most successful, powerful, generous people who've been in your shoes. Heed their advice! If you do, you just might end up discovering that following founders is your specialty. Like Simon Freakley, Bruce Chizen, and Alex Shootman, you might engineer your own exit and do it all again and again.

As for me, guiding SBI through two transactions that allowed the original four partners to exit day-to-day operations was a joy and one of the highlights of my life. But I don't plan to follow another founder. I've been enjoying post-CEO life for two years, coaching Second CEOs through their transitions. And what began as a desire to make what I know and do more widely available has turned into my next chapter: a coaching and advisory platform for current or potential Second CEOs.

A Final Word . . .

High achievers have a tendency to always focus on mistakes. Before you start spending time looking at what you didn't do, I want you to spend a little bit of time sitting in the bleachers and observing yourself. Being on the floor, engaged in the game, can wait a moment. Sit back. You're in a position that a minuscule percentage of individuals ever get to. I know everything isn't perfect, but please take time to recognize you probably grew or will grow more in the first year than in the previous decade. This role does that to you; it makes you grow.

For those thinking about Year One versus Year Two, let me help you anticipate what's coming. How do you have a great Year Two? By helping the business make a massive leap toward achieving your Horizon Two VCP. Remember, your role exists to accelerate scale. Following a founder often means you're professionalizing the business. Not because it wasn't professional before, but because you have a different lens and a different job to do.

You're never done when you're the CEO of a business, especially one that was led by a founder. There are always going to be things that you recognize you need to be doing differently. Instead of getting frustrated about what those things are, embrace the fact that being a top-tier CEO is like having a hobby, where you're always building things and you're never finished.

We never reach our full potential—none of us. We're all always works-in-progress. The trick is in knowing you'll never reach your full potential but always moving toward it. *How do you do that?* By carving out time to reflect on your journey, appreciate it, and also recognize there are the new things you're going to need to bring to the table.

There are three things the CEO will *always* be responsible for: (1) vision/strategy, (2) culture, and (3) team. You must continue to invest in these three components and never delegate them. They're *your* priorities.

You're more than good enough. The team is following you/will follow you.

There are no straight lines when it comes to success. Success is a winding road with a series of U-turns. But you're in a camp of individuals now, from a business perspective, that nobody will ever be able to take away from you.

People are ready to follow you when you put yourself in a position to be one who influences—not demands. The CEO role is not about control; in fact, it's the opposite. The sooner you realize that, the more successful you will be. The further you move up, the less control you have, but the more *influence* you will have. You have the ability to change people's lives in a meaningful way. Talk about impact!

To step toward your full potential in the role of the CEO is to realize that regardless of industry, you're in one business: the people business. People will be at the center of your results, good or bad. So, keep investing in being in the top 1 percent of leading and influencing others. Helping others get what they want will get you what you want.

Congratulations. Keep betting on yourself. And remember, in the journey to full potential, you're never, ever done.

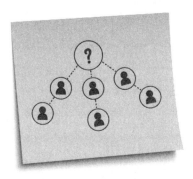

ABOUT THE AUTHOR

Matt Sharrers is the managing partner of ETJ Advisory, a firm he and his wife started in 2020. Matt is a CEO coach, investor, and board advisor. He specializes in coaching PE backed CEOs and serving on the boards of these companies. Matt currently serves on six boards. Prior to starting ETJ, Matt was the first employee of SBI, a B2B strategy consulting firm that specializes in growth. Matt joined the cofounders in 2008 and was CEO from 2017 to 2022, guiding the firm through two private equity transactions. Prior to SBI, he spent a decade at Cintas in a variety of sales roles. Matt played professional hockey directly out of college before starting his business career.

Philanthropically, Matt and Lynne run ETJ Athletics. ETJ Athletics' purpose is to enable young women and men to reach their full potential in athletics. They currently sponsor elite athletes in MMA, wrestling, hockey (players and officials), and swimming.

Matt and Lynne are the proud parents of four young adults. When not traveling, they are both very active, participating in a series of outdoor adventure races, regular boxing, and just enough golf to keep you addicted. Matt and Lynne live in Scottsdale, Arizona.